P-38 LIGHTNING
VS
Bf 109

North Africa, Sicily and Italy 1942–43

EDWARD M. YOUNG

OSPREY

Bloomsbury Publishing Plc

Kemp House, Chawley Park, Cumnor Hill, Oxford, OX2 9PH, UK

29 Earlsfort Terrace, Dublin 2, Ireland

1385 Broadway, 5th Floor, New York, NY 10018, USA

E-mail: info@ospreypublishing.com

www.ospreypublishing.com

OSPREY is a trademark of Osprey Publishing Ltd

First published in Great Britain in 2023

A catalogue record for this book is available from the British Library.

ISBN: PB: 9781472859549; eBook 9781472859532; ePDF 9781472859525; XML 9781472859556

23 24 25 26 27 10 9 8 7 6 5 4 3 2 1

Edited by Tony Holmes
Cover artwork and battlescene by Gareth Hector
Three-views, cockpit views, Engaging the Enemy and armament views by Jim Laurier
Map and tactical diagrams by www.bounford.com
Index by Fionbar Lyons
Typeset by PDQ Digital Media Solutions, Bungay, UK
Printed and bound in India by Replika Press Private Ltd.

Osprey Publishing supports the Woodland Trust, the UK's leading woodland conservation charity.

To find out more about our authors and books visit **www.ospreypublishing.com**. Here you will find extracts, author interviews, details of forthcoming events and the option to sign up for our newsletter.

Acknowledgments

In preparing this volume, I have relied on the works by Christopher Shores and his colleagues, Jochen Prien and his colleagues and the detailed research of the late Frank Oylnyk, all cited in the Selected Reading at the end of the book. Their compilations of Allied and Axis claims and losses formed the basis for this study. I would like to thank Nicole Davis at the Museum of Flight for permission to use photographs from the John Lambert Collection and Debbie Seracini at the San Diego Air & Space Museum for permission to use photographs from their collection. The staff at the Still Pictures Branch at the National Archives in College Park, Maryland, provided excellent support. Tammy Horton at the Air Force Historical Research Agency, Maxwell AFB, Alabama, responded to numerous requests for group and squadron records. I would like to thank Gareth Hector and Jim Laurier for their excellent artwork, and my editor, Tony Holmes, for responding positively to the idea for this Duel volume, and for his encouragement.

P-38 Lightning cover artwork

On December 2, 1942, Capt Newell Roberts led four P-38s from the 1st FG's 94th FS on a mission to strafe targets in southern Tunisia. After attacking several trucks, the flight continued on to the Luftwaffe airfield at Gabes, where they saw four Bf 109s (from 5./JG 51) taking off. The Lightnings came in right behind the German fighters, and future ace 1Lt Jack Ilfrey (flying his assigned P-38F, 41-7587) fired on one of the Bf 109s at close range and saw the aircraft's wingtip hit the ground. The Messerschmitt cartwheeled away in flames. More enemy fighters had by then taken off, attacking the P-38s and knocking out the right engine of Ilfrey's Lightning. Although he lost his radio in another attack, Ilfrey was rescued by two fellow pilots from his squadron, who escorted him back to their airfield at Nouvion, in Algeria. (Artwork by Gareth Hector)

Bf 109 cover artwork

Bf 109G-6 "Black 2" was the mount of ace Oberfeldwebel Herbert Rollwage, assigned to 5./JG 53, who flew the fighter in combat during the doomed defense of Sicily in July 1943. Seven months earlier, in December 1942, Rollwage had claimed four P-38s shot down over Tunisia, and he destroyed a fifth on July 10, 1943 – the day of the Allied invasion of Sicily – for his 45th victory. Later that same day Rollwage was shot down and wounded in combat with Allied fighters. He did not claim any more victories until January 7, 1944, when he was credited with the destruction of two P-38s over Graz, in Austria. Rollwage's tally stood at 66 victories by war's end. (Artwork by Gareth Hector)

Previous Page

Pilots from the 96th FS/82nd FG who claimed 16 Axis fighters over Sardinia on June 18, 1943. Future nine-victory ace Flt Off Frank Hurlbut, kneeling second from right, claimed one Bf 109 shot down and one damaged, as well as a Re.2001 destroyed. (3A-28938, RG 342FH, National Archives and Records Administration (NARA))

CONTENTS

INTRODUCTION

In his study of the air campaign in North Africa, Sicily and Italy during 1942–43 (see Further Reading), Christopher Rein states that the P-38 Lightning was "the most valuable fighter sent to North Africa. Lockheed's unique twin-boom design provided something no other nation could match – a twin-engined fighter that was maneuverable enough to hold its own in combat with the best single-engined fighters, yet had the endurance to perform long-range escort missions".

The P-38's greatest contribution to the Allied campaign was as an escort fighter to the US Army Air Force (USAAF) heavy and medium bombers assigned to the Twelfth Air Force. While its value as an escort fighter is beyond dispute, more recent research into Allied and Axis claims for enemy aircraft destroyed compared to actual losses suggests that the accepted narrative of the Lightning's success against German single-engined fighters like the Messerschmitt Bf 109 may need to be revised. Far from holding its own in combat with the Bf 109, during the 1942–43 air campaign in the Mediterranean USAAF P-38 units may well have suffered a loss rate of three-to-one in favor of the German fighter.

The war for North Africa, and the subsequent invasions of Sicily and Italy, can be seen as a battle of logistics. During World War II, in periods of intense fighting, Allied and Axis armies and air forces consumed supplies at prodigious rates. Both sides needed steady and secure flows of men and equipment, aircraft and vehicles, fuel, food, ammunition, spare parts and a host of other items to continue in combat.

For a period after the initial invasion of North Africa on November 8, 1942, the Axis forces held the advantage. The German and Italian forces fighting in Tunisia depended on a comparatively short line of communications running from ports and airfields in Sicily and Italy to Bizerte and Tunis, the main ports in Tunisia, and airfields nearby. This enabled the Germans to rapidly send reinforcements to Tunisia to counter the Allied invasion. In contrast, British and American forces had to depend on a much longer line of communications. Supplies had to come principally by ship from Britain and across the Atlantic from the United States.

It took some months for the Allies to build up the logistical infrastructure in Morocco and Algeria to support a sustained air and ground offensive against Axis forces in Tunisia. Axis supply lines were, however, vulnerable to attack long before that. All the principal port facilities, marshaling yards and airfields in Tunisia, Sardinia, Sicily and southern Italy were in range of Allied aircraft, while Axis shipping and air transports could and did come under attack while en route to Tunisia. The heavy and medium bombers of the Royal Air Force (RAF) and the USAAF's Ninth and Twelfth Air Forces carried out an intensive and successful aerial interdiction campaign against Axis supplies and supply lines to Tunisia.

After defeating the Axis in Tunisia, the Allied air forces turned their attention to disrupting the lines of communication in Sicily and southern Italy and to neutralizing Axis air power prior to the invasion of Sicily. Escorting the Twelfth Air Force bombers became the principal mission of the three P-38 fighter groups (1st, 14th and 82nd FGs) assigned to the Twelfth. Conversely, the defense of these vital targets from Allied air attacks fell primarily to the Luftwaffe, and specifically the *Jagdgruppen* (Fighter Groups) of *Luftflotte* (Air Fleet) 2 equipped with the Bf 109.

The invasion of North Africa saw the first aerial clashes between the P-38 – the USAAF's premier fighter at that time – and the venerable Bf 109, early versions of which had already been in combat for more than five years. The duels between the P-38s and the Bf 109s over Tunisia, Sardinia, Sicily and Italy would be fierce battles between aircraft of roughly comparable performance and pilots of unequal experience. American bomber escort tactics, certain flying characteristics of the P-38 and the difference in combat experience between American and German aviators would often give the advantage in combat to the Bf 109 pilots.

Although they had some similarities, the Bf 109 and the P-38 were designed to meet different requirements. Both had nose-mounted armament and were powered

Pilots from the 49th FS/14th FG come together for a group photograph at Hamilton Field, in California, in June 1942. The unit trained here prior to heading to England at the end of the following month. By the end of January 1943, five of these young pilots had been killed in action or captured. Standing first left in the second row is 2Lt Richard I. Bong, who would soon depart for the Southwest Pacific, and fame, as America's leading fighter ace of World War II. (2011-06-25 image_013_01, John Lambert Collection, Museum of Flight (MoF))

Feldwebel Anton Hafner poses with his Bf 109G shortly after arriving in Tunisia in November 1942 as a member of 6./JG 51. Hafner was one of the Luftwaffe *Experten* who exacted a heavy toll on the P-38 units, claiming eight Lightnings between November 30, 1942 and January 2, 1943. Prior to 6./JG 51's transfer to Tunisia, Hafner had been credited with 62 Soviet aircraft destroyed on the Eastern Front. He had claimed 203 victories by the time he was killed in action on October 17, 1944 whilst flying his 795th operational sortie. (Bundesarchiv (B.A.) Bild 1011-418-1841-31A)

by liquid-cooled, inline engines. Messerschmitt's fighter, however, was intended to meet the Luftwaffe's need for a short-range, tactical fighter that could wrest air superiority from an opposing air force and escort Luftwaffe bombers and attack aircraft on their missions against tactical targets. The Bf 109's initial armament of two rifle-caliber machine guns was not atypical of fighters of the time.

The P-38, in contrast, was intended as an interceptor, with the speed, rate of climb, range and heavy armament necessary to destroy enemy bombers. At a time when many American pursuits had one 0.30-cal. and one 0.50-cal. machine gun mounted in the nose, the mixed cannon and four machine gun armament of the Lightning was a radical innovation. The P-38 was large for a fighter of the era, weighing twice as much as the Bf 109 and with a wingspan that was 60 percent greater. This combination meant that achieving a high rate of roll required high control forces. It appears that this may have proved to be a deficiency in the type of air combat the P-38 engaged in over North Africa, Sicily and Italy against the Bf 109.

The greater disparity between P-38 and Bf 109 pilots, at least in the initial months of combat, was the difference in combat experience. Lightning pilots arrived in North Africa at the end of 1942 with no experience of air combat. They would find that some of the formations they had flown in training were not well suited to doing battle with Axis fighters. They had to work out the best tactics for achieving what became their primary mission – escorting American bombers to and from their targets. There were lessons that had to be learned, sometimes at great cost. The P-38 groups did develop new tactics, and despite their losses, they proved their worth as long-range escort fighters, providing excellent protection to the bombers.

In contrast, many of the Bf 109 pilots in the *Jagdgruppen* who flew over North Africa, Sicily, and Italy were highly experienced in air combat. The elite pilots, the *Experten*, had in some cases flown for more than two years against the Royal Air Force (RAF) and the Soviet Red Army Air Force, during which time many of them had amassed record numbers of victory claims. For the Bf 109 pilots who were credited with five or more P-38s shot down during 1942–43, their average number of victories prior to their first claim for a Lightning was 44. There was also another class of pilot that the Luftwaffe referred to as the *"Alte Hasen"* ("old hares"). These men may not have had the very high scores of the *Experten*, but they were highly experienced and equally as dangerous. The German pilots had honed their tactics in hundreds of aerial battles.

While the Bf 109 pilots would prove successful in combat with the P-38s, theirs was something of a pyrrhic victory – not in terms of the aircraft they lost in combat, but in their inability to prevent the serious damage American bombers, with their Lightning escorts, inflicted on the Axis in the Mediterranean during 1942–43.

CHRONOLOGY

1934

February   *Reichsluftministerium* (RLM) issues a development contract to Messerschmitt for a new day fighter, designated Bf 109.

1935

May 29   First flight of the Bf 109 V1.

1936

February–March   Competitive trials between the Bf 109 and the Heinkel He 112

carried out at Travemünde. RLM selects the Bf 109 as the Luftwaffe's next day fighter.

Fall   Messerschmitt begins preparations for Bf 109 production.

1937

February   The US Army Air Corps (USAAC) issues Circular Proposal X-608 calling for a fighter capable of intercepting enemy bombers at high altitude.

The P-38 production line at the Lockheed factory in Burbank, California, where all Lightnings were constructed during the war. It took time to build the P-38 in meaningful numbers, Lockheed completing 205 in 1941, 1,264 in 1942 and 2,213 in 1943. Overseas theaters and newly formed P-38 units had priority, leaving few aircraft available for transition training well into 1943. (Bilstein 00726, San Diego Air & Space Museum (SDASM))

February	Messerschmitt begins delivery of the Bf 109B to the Luftwaffe's JG 132.
April	Lockheed submits its Model 22 design for the X-608 proposal.
June	The USAAC orders a prototype of the Model 22 as the XP-38.
December	Bf 109 V15 (prototype of the Bf 109E) fitted with a Daimler-Benz DB 601A engine makes its first flight.

1938

January	Tests begin on the improved Bf 109E with the DB 601A engine.
December	Bf 109E enters service with the Luftwaffe.

1939

January 27	1Lt (later Brig Gen) Benjamin S. Kelsey makes the first flight of the XP-38.
April 27	USAAC places an order with Lockheed for 13 YP-38 service test aircraft.

1940

May 4	Anglo-French Purchasing Commission places an order with Lockheed for 667 Model 322-61s – export version of the P-38 without turbosuperchargers – named Lightning I.
August	Production of the Bf 109F-1 commences.
August 30	USAAC orders 607 P-38s.
September	First flights of the YP-38.

1941

January 15	14th Pursuit Group (PG) activated.
July 1	First of 36 P-38Ds delivered to the USAAC. Aircraft assigned to the 1st PG's 27th Pursuit Squadron (PS).
November	Lockheed begins production of the P-38E.
December	1st PG moves to San Diego to provide air defense of southern California with six YP-38s, 23 P-38s and 19 P-38Ds.

1942

February 9	82nd PG activated.
February	14th PG begins converting to the P-38, followed by the 82nd PG
March	Lockheed begins delivery of improved P-38F to the USAAF. These progressively replace earlier P-38D/Es with the 1st, 14th and 82nd PGs.
May	All USAAF pursuit groups redesignated fighter groups (FGs).
June	Bf 109G-1 and G-2 enter service with the Luftwaffe.
June–August	1st and 14th FGs move to England for assignment to the Eighth Air Force.
August 20	Twelfth Air Force activated to provide air support for Operation *Torch* invasion of Vichy French North Africa.
September –October	82nd FG moves to England.
September –November	*Jagdgruppen* in the Mediterranean re-equip with Bf 109G-2s.
November 10	Operation *Torch* sees Allied landings at Casablanca, in Morocco, and Oran and Algiers, in Algeria.
November 10–14	The Luftwaffe rapidly sends reinforcements to Tunisia, including the Bf 109-equipped II./JG 51 and II. and III./JG 53.
November 12–14	1st and 14th FGs fly directly from England to North Africa, joining the Twelfth Air Force.
November 28	First combat between P-38s and Bf 109s. On a fighter sweep to Bizerte, Bf 109s from II./JG 53 attack P-38s from the 14th FG's 48th and 49th Fighter Squadrons (FSs), downing one P-38 from each squadron and damaging two more.

November 30	P-38 pilots from the 1st and 14th FGs make their first claims for Bf 109s shot down, claiming two destroyed and two probables for the loss of one 14th FG P-38. II./JG 51 loses one Bf 109, while II./JG 53 has one damaged.
December	82nd FG flies from England to North Africa.

1943

January	After suffering heavy losses in aircraft and pilots, the 14th FG is withdrawn from combat.
January	The Mediterranean *Jagdgruppen* begin receiving Bf 109G-4s.
February 18	Activation of the Mediterranean Allied Air Forces (MAAF). 1st and 82nd FGs are assigned to the Northwest African Strategic Air Force (NASAF) under the command of Brig Gen James Doolittle.
February 19–24	Battle of Kasserine Pass
March	The *Jagdgruppen* begin replacing Bf 109G-2 and G-4 with the Bf 109G-6.
April 5	Beginning of Operation *Flax* sweeps against Axis transport aircraft flying supplies to Tunisia.
May	14th FG returns to combat.

May 13	All Axis forces in Tunisia surrender.
May–June	NASAF heavy and medium bombers, with P-38 escorts, intensify attacks on Axis airfields, ports and marshaling yards in Sicily and southern Italy.
July 10	Sicily invaded (Operation *Husky*).
August	P-38s continue escorting heavy and medium bombers in attacks on southern Italy. On August 30, the 1st FG loses 13 P-38s in combat with Bf 109s while defending bombers, which suffer no losses. 1st FG is awarded a Distinguished Unit Citation (DUC) following this mission.
September 2	82nd FG loses nine P-38s in combat with Bf 109s while escorting bombers. Again, no bombers are lost. 82nd is also awarded a DUC.
September 9	Operation *Avalanche* (invasion of Italy) begins, with Allied troops landing at Salerno.
November 1	Fifteenth Air Force activated for strategic bombing of targets in southern Europe. 1st, 14th and 82nd FGs transferred from Twelfth to Fifteenth Air Force control.

A production line of Bf 109G-6 fighters at one of several factories that built the Bf 109 during the war. Messerschmitt had factories in Germany manufacturing the Bf 109 and contracted with Erla Maschinenwerk and Wiener Neustädter Flugzeugwerk (W.N.F.) in Austria for additional production. During 1944 these three companies built more than 14,000 Bf 109s. (B.A. Bild 1011-638-4221-06)

DESIGN AND DEVELOPMENT

P-38F/G LIGHTNING

The XP-38 made its first flight on January 27, 1939. It would take nearly three years for Lockheed to produce a combat-ready aircraft and begin quantity production. The XP-38 was not just a radical design, it was a big and complicated aircraft, larger and heavier than any other American pursuit of the time, with two engines, two turbosupercharger systems and a tricycle landing gear. It would prove to be the most expensive American fighter of World War II, costing nearly twice as much as the North American P-51 Mustang to produce. Despite the crash of the prototype in February 1939, the USAAC had enough confidence in Lockheed's design to place an order in April for 13 YP-38 service test aircraft. This was followed in September by a contract for 66 P-38s.

The YP-38 was a different aircraft from the XP-38. To prepare the fighter for quantity production, Lockheed made substantial changes in its structure, as well as incorporating improvements derived from the limited flight testing of the XP-38. The biggest change was the shift from the Allison V-1710C engine to the V-1710F (V-1710-27/29 (F2R/L)). As the P-38 featured counter-rotating propellers, one was designated as the left engine and one as the right engine. While producing the same 1,150hp as the V-1710C, the F series had a higher thrust line, necessitating a revised engine cowling and new forged mounts to replace the tubular engine mounts in the XP-38.

Following initial flight testing of the XP-38, legendary Lockheed designer Clarence "Kelly" Johnson had recommended changes to the Prestone cooling radiators, an improved turbosupercharger installation, revised oil cooler inlets and exhaust cooling ducts and a seven square foot increase in the horizontal stabilizer area.

The USAAC also requested a change in the proposed armament. The XP-38 was to have been fitted with a 23mm Danish Madsen cannon with 50 rounds, and four 0.50-cal.

The first YP-38 around the time of its maiden flight in public on September 20, 1940. Note the dummy "machine guns" mounted in the nose for the benefit of the media. Impressed with the XP-38's performance despite its destruction only a few weeks after its first flight, the USAAC ordered 13 YP-38s in April 1939. (16_008100, SDASM)

machine guns with 200 rounds each. For the YP-38, the USAAC wanted a Browning M9 37mm cannon with a 15 round magazine, two 0.50-cal. machine guns with 200 rounds per gun and two 0.30-cal. machine guns with 500 rounds per gun. In early August 1940, shortly before the first flight of the YP-38, the USAAC changed the configuration to four 0.50-cal. machine guns in addition to the 37mm cannon. Lockheed later claimed that more than 30,000 changes had to be made to get the P-38 ready for production, rendering nearly $1 million worth of production machinery and equipment obsolete.

In August 1940, the USAAC's Commanding General, Maj Gen Henry H. "Hap" Arnold, visited the Lockheed factory in Los Angeles to view the first YP-38 before its maiden flight. Arnold claimed that the Lockheed "interceptor," as it was referred to in the press, was the world's fastest military aircraft, and could attain a speed of 460mph "at two-thirds throttle" – a bit of an exaggeration. The YP-38 undertook its first flight on September 17, 1940. Three days later, the aircraft made its first public flight for the local press, with *The Los Angeles Times* reporting that Lockheed's "deadly new interceptor pursuit plane" flashed across the airfield "scorching out of the haze like a triple-headed hornet."

As they slowly emerged from production, the YP-38s underwent intensive testing at Lockheed and with USAAC pilots, with the first YP-38 remaining with the manufacturer and the second going to Wright Field, in Ohio, on January 28, 1941. Seven were then supplied to the 1st PG at Selfridge Field, in Michigan, for service testing. Most lacked armament, but at least one YP-38 went to Selfridge Field for testing with a Browning 37mm cannon installed. The USAAC had, apparently, already decided to replace the 37mm cannon with the smaller 20mm cannon on later versions. One Hispano M1 20mm cannon and four Browning M2 0.50-cal. machine guns would become standard armament for all subsequent P-38 models.

While working simultaneously on a larger order for a modified P-38, designated the Model P-322, for the British (who gave the name Lightning to the new fighter), Lockheed began turning out P-38 and P-38D aircraft under the first production order. It completed 29 P-38s between June and August 1941, and these aircraft still had provision for the 37mm cannon, although not all were fitted with armament.

The P-38D, shown here, followed the P-38 in production – the USAAC inexplicably skipped the B and C designations. The P-38D had armor protection for the pilot, bullet-proof glass and self-sealing fuel tanks. Some, but not all, of the P-38Ds had an armament of four 0.50-cal. machine guns. Most went to the 1st, 14th, 78th and 82nd PGs as training aircraft. (15_002805 SDASM)

OPPOSITE

P-38F-1 Lightning 41-7498 was assigned to Capt Newell Roberts of the 94th FS/1st FG in late November 1942, and he flew this aircraft until he completed his required quota of missions in March 1943. During his time in combat, Roberts claimed four Bf 109s destroyed, a fifth as a probable and a sixth damaged, in addition to half-shares in an Bf 110 and a Cant Z.1007. 2Lt James Hagenback took over the fighter following Roberts' departure, and he named it *BAT OUT OF HELL*. Hagenback claimed an additional Bf 109 damaged, an Fw 190 and a C.200 as probables and a third-share in the destruction of an SM.82 in combat over Sicily.

Based on information coming from USAAC observers in Britain, Lockheed added self-sealing fuel tanks and armor protection for the pilot to the P-38D, 36 of which were delivered between August and October 1941 – many went to the 1st PG. In the P-38 and P-38D, Lockheed replaced the curved front windscreen of the YP-38 with a framed windscreen that had a flat, bullet-resistant panel inside. A gun camera was also installed in the nose.

The P-38E was the first model of the Lightning to enter combat. Retaining the Allison V-1710-27/29, rated at 1,150hp for take-off, the P-38E incorporated some 2,000 alterations – principally better electrical and hydraulic systems and improved radios and flight instruments. It also had a redesigned nose undercarriage, which saw the drag strut that had been located forward of the main strut shifted to its rear, thus allowing more space in the nose compartment for additional ammunition for the four 0.50-cal. machine guns. To accommodate the larger supply of rounds, the machine guns were now staggered, with the barrels projecting at different lengths.

Early on in production, Lockheed added a rear-view mirror above the canopy. It built 210 P-38Es, and these began to equip the 1st, 14th, and 82nd PGs (changed to fighter groups in May 1942) for the defense of the American West Coast after the attack on Pearl Harbor. The 54th FS took its P-38Es to Alaska, and on 4 August 1942 two Lightning pilots claimed two Japanese Type 97 Flying Boats shot down over the Aleutians for the first P-38 victories of World War II.

As Daimler-Benz would do with its engines for the Bf 109, Allison managed to obtain incremental increases in power out of the V-1710 as the war progressed. Like the DB 600 series, the Allison V-1710 was a liquid-cooled, 12-cylinder, inline engine, although not inverted like the German powerplant. In the early 1930s, after General Motors purchased the company, Allison continued development of the V-1710. The first USAAC fighter to employ it was the Curtiss XP-37, followed by the Bell XFM-1/YFM-1. By 1940, Allison V-1710s not only powered the XP-38, but also the Bell XP-39 and the Curtiss XP-40, with the V-1710C series giving 1,040hp to 1,150hp for take-off. The first of the improved V-1710F series maintained the same power output, but Allison continued working on the engine to boost this further. With the V-1710F-5, Allison added an improved engine-stage supercharger and other features

P-38F-1 LIGHTNING

37ft 10in.

17498

UNC

12ft 10in.

52ft 0in.

that strengthened the internal structure of the engine to allow for 1,325hp for take-off and 1,150hp at 25,000ft.

The P-38F, which entered production in March 1942, was the first model equipped with the V-1710F-5 as the V-1710-49/53 (F5R/L). The increase in power, however, proved too great for the P-38's intercooler system. Air coming out of a turbosupercharger is hot and needs to be cooled before it can enter the carburettor through the intercooler. The intercooler system Lockheed designed was ingenious, but it proved to be inefficient. On the early models of the P-38 the intercoolers were located in the leading edge of the wing. Hot air from the turbosuperchargers went to the wing leading edge to be cooled, before flowing back to the engine carburettors. The intercooling system was designed for an Allison engine giving 1,150hp, and the extra power of the V-1710-49/53 created carburettor air temperatures that were too high. Therefore, in order to avoid engine problems, pilots had to reduce take-off and military power ratings from 1,325hp to 1,150hp, particularly at high altitudes. Later, in October 1942, the recommended ratings were increased to 1,340hp for take-off and 1,240hp for military power.

In other respects the P-38F was similar to the P-38E, with various minor improvements such as switching the pitot tube from under the nose to under the port wing, allowing the antenna mast to be moved under the nose. The P-38F had a pylon under each inboard wing section to carry a 165-gallon drop tank. Beginning with the P-38F-15, Lockheed introduced a mechanism that allowed the Lightning's Fowler flaps to be partially extended at airspeeds below 250mph. These were called 'combat' or maneuvering flaps.

Lockheed began building the next model, the P-38G, in August 1942. Similar in form to the P-38F, the most important change was a shift to the V-1710-51/55 (F10R/L) engine, which featured a larger carburettor and higher supercharger gear ratings that allowed for higher power ratings, giving a slight increase in top speed at 25,000ft over the P-38F. The turbosupercharger was changed to the General Electric Type B-13, an improvement over the earlier Type B-2. The P-38G series had a strengthened center section to allow for heavier drop tanks and bombs, the pylons being capable of carrying a 300-gallon drop tank or a 2,000lb bomb. P-38F/Gs would be the first Lightnings to confront Luftwaffe fighters over North Africa and the Mediterranean.

The P-38F was the first model to be truly combat-capable, and it was also the first Lightning to see action in North Africa after examples were flown across the Atlantic to Britain and then from Britain to Algeria. The P-38F had the now-standard armament of one 20mm cannon and four 0.50-cal. machine guns, and it could carry two drop tanks or bombs on pylons under each inboard wing section. (98255, Record Group 18WP, NARA)

There were three attributes of the early-model P-38s that appear to have affected the Lightning's performance in aerial combat against the Bf 109 – compressibility, restrictions on full military power at altitude, as previously described, and rate of roll.

The P-38 was the first American fighter aircraft to experience compressibility when diving from high altitudes. In diving, a P-38 pilot would encounter buffeting and, as speed increased, a tendency for the aircraft to tuck under into a more vertical dive – the phenomenon appeared to be more pronounced at altitudes above 25,000ft. To avoid compressibility, P-38F/G pilots were given diving speed limits of no more than 290mph at 30,000ft and 370mph at 25,000ft, and cautioned not to exceed these limits. This caution did not go unnoticed. Thirty-nine-victory ace Leutnant Johann Pichler, a Bf 109 pilot who flew over North Africa with 7./JG 77 in 1942–43 and who claimed two P-38s in aerial combat, found that:

> . . . an excellent means of breaking off combat was to go into a power dive from high altitude. The P-38 pilots rarely followed us. At first we could not understand this, but the mystery was explained a few months later when a captured P-38 pilot told us that in a dive, the aircraft became too fast to be pulled out safely.

Leutnant Johann Pichler of 7./JG 77 claimed two P-38s destroyed in June 1943, the 39-victory ace encountering the Lightning on numerous occasions during the final months of the campaign in North Africa and the ill-fated defense of Sicily. A veteran of more than 700 operational sorties and a recipient of the Knight's Cross, Pichler was badly wounded in combat with USAAF fighters over Rumania on July 28, 1944 and subsequently captured by Soviet troops whilst still in hospital. He eventually returned to Germany in 1950. (Tony Holmes Collection)

The P-38 was intended to be an interceptor capable of downing enemy bombers at high altitudes using a fast rate of climb and high speed. It was not designed for fighter-versus-fighter combat, although it proved capable of doing so in the right circumstances. In order to meet USAAC requirements, Lockheed had to use two engines, which resulted in a large aircraft with a large wingspan. As Brig Gen Benjamin S. Kelsey (the XP-38's test pilot, who was subsequently instrumental in its development into a frontline fighter) explained:

> Rolling in and out of turns with alacrity is an essential factor in maneuvering fighters. Therefore, rate of roll becomes a major consideration. A large wingspan tends to degrade a plane's rolling rate because the wing surface is so far out from the fuselage and center of gravity. Making the wingtips narrower by tapering the planform helps. The P-38 had a taper ratio of three, with the tip being only one-third as wide as its root. Normal configurations would have had a taper ratio of about two. This tended to offset what might have been expected to be a serious rolling rate disadvantage of a large-span plane.

Still, while the P-38 had an equal or shorter turn radius than comparable American fighters of the time, it had a slower rate of roll. A report on tests with the P-39D, P-40F and P-51A concluded that:

> In the initial turn, due to the slowness of aileron roll of the P-38F, the other types could roll into a turn faster and close up the circle rapidly before the P-38F would reach its maximum radius of turn. It would then take the P-38F some time, if ever, to overcome this initial disadvantage.

As Col Royal D. Frey, who flew P-38s with the 20th FG from England, recalled:

Although the P-38 could turn very tightly once it got into a bank, getting it into a bank was another matter. Late J series and L series Lightnings had aileron boost, but this feature came too late for those few of us who took on the Luftwaffe deep inside Germany in those grim days of late 1943 and early 1944. Because of the weight of the plane and the poor leverage of a control wheel compared to that of a control stick, the plane's roll rate approximated that of a pregnant whale. If we ever got behind a single-engined fighter in a tight turn, all the other pilot had to do was flip into an opposite turn and dive; by the time we had banked and turned after him, he was practically out of sight.

Bf 109G

By the end of 1942, the Luftwaffe was facing not just accelerating attrition, but growing demands on three fronts – in the West, the East and the Mediterranean. The German fighter force had, by the end of October, lost 115 percent of its strength available in January to enemy action and operational accidents. Fighter aircraft written off amounted to 1,734, with an additional 1,486 aircraft damaged. During the year fighter production had increased dramatically, but Britain and America were already building two-and-a-half times as many fighters as Germany, and American production was still accelerating.

As American historian and author Williamson Murray has noted, Hitler's decision to contest the Allied invasion of North Africa while maintaining the Wehrmacht's commitments on the Eastern Front was, for the Luftwaffe, a catastrophe. In the circumstances, the German aircraft industry had no alternative but to accelerate production of existing aircraft types. For the fighter force, this meant continuing a heavy reliance on the Bf 109, as the newer Focke-Wulf Fw 190 was still experiencing

The story of the Bf 109 is one of progressive engine development. Messerschmitt originally designed the fighter to be powered by the Junkers Jumo 210 or the Daimler DB 600, with the latter engine then still under development. The Bf 109B, shown here, was equipped with a Jumo 210 rated at 680hp for take-off, giving the aircraft a maximum speed of 289mph at 13,120ft. (Author's Collection)

technical problems. For the design team at Messerschmitt, the challenge was to find ways of improving the Bf 109's performance to meet the ever-changing demands of aerial combat.

The Bf 109 made its first flight in September 1935 and entered combat with the *Legion Condor* in Spain in early 1937. As the Luftwaffe's premier single-seat fighter, the Bf 109 had participated in every air campaign since the start of the war in Europe. Fortuitously for the Luftwaffe, the Bf 109 proved highly adaptable to fitting engines of greater power so that its performance could keep pace with opposing fighters. The Bf 109 was designed to use either the 680hp Junkers Jumo 210 or the 960hp Daimler-Benz DB 600Aa, both of which were liquid-cooled, 12-cylinder inverted inline engines. As the DB 600 was still under development, the Jumo engine would power the first production series of the Messerschmitt fighter, the Bf 109B, and the subsequent C- and D-models.

The Bf 109E series employed the Daimler-Benz DB 601A inverted-vee liquid-cooled 12-cylinder engine (now driving a three-bladed VDM propeller) giving 1,175hp for take-off in the Bf 109E-3. The new engine required a complete re-design of the nose, placement of radiators under each wing and the addition of an air intake on the port side ahead of the cockpit. (Tony Holmes Collection)

It is remarkable that the first production model, the Bf 109B, had an engine providing just 680hp for take-off, while the final model, the Bf 109K, had an engine developing 2,000hp – three times greater in the same basic airframe. This evolution in engine power came about through intensive efforts to develop the DB 600 series, with Daimler-Benz proving able to incrementally boost the power output as the war progressed.

In the early 1930s Daimler-Benz was working on an experimental liquid-cooled, inverted 12-cylinder aircraft engine designated the F4. This engine had a carburettor fuel system, water cooling and separate cylinders. For the renamed DB 600 engine, Daimler-Benz switched to monobloc construction to strengthen the engine, added a large supercharger on its left side, but retained the carburettor fuel system. During 1936 the DB 600 evolved into the DB 601 when Daimler-Benz replaced the carburettor fuel system with direct fuel injection to the cylinders, increased the compression ratio from 6.5 to 6.9 and improved the supercharger drive system. The DB 601 underwent intensive testing during 1936–37, and it was not until the summer of 1938 that the engine was fitted to the Bf 109 when the V14 and V15 carried out tests with it.

The DB 601 was longer and substantially heavier than the Jumo 210, necessitating a major redesign of the Bf 109. The supercharger air intake was moved from the upper starboard side of the nose to a position on the port side. The large coolant radiator common to the Jumo-powered versions was replaced with a smaller oil cooler, reshaping the nose profile, and with two rectangular coolant radiators located under the wings. The new model had a three-bladed propeller.

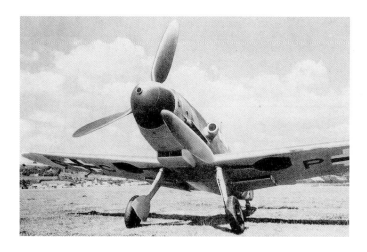

With the DB 601A rated at 1,050hp for take-off and 1,100hp at 12,140ft, maximum speed jumped from 289mph at 13,120ft to 342mph, with similar improvements in climb rate. Deliveries of the new Bf 109E series began in early 1939. Later, Daimler-Benz introduced the DB 601N, which produced 1,270hp using 100 octane fuel. This engine powered some of the later E series aircraft.

The promise of Daimler-Benz engines of greater power and the need to continue improving the Bf 109's performance led to another thorough redesign of the Messerschmitt fighter as the Bf 109F. It incorporated several aerodynamic refinements to take advantage of newly developed Daimler-Benz engines. The engine cowling was deepened and made more symmetrical, with a larger propeller spinner that would characterize all subsequent models. Rounded wingtips replaced the square tips of the earlier Bf 109B, C, D and E, and the struts bracing the tail were removed. The underwing radiators, which had been a source of drag on the E-model, were refined, recessing them further into the wings and changing the flow of cooling air.

The F series dispensed with the wing-mounted 20mm cannon and concentrated armament in the nose, replacing the MG FF cannon with a single MG 151 15mm or 20mm cannon mounted in the engine and firing through the hollow propeller shaft, while retaining the two MG 17 7.9mm machine guns.

The DB 601N powered the Bf 109F-1 and F-2 series, but Daimler-Benz later introduced the DB 601E, which followed the DB 601N. The DB 601E developed 1,350hp for take-off. This engine, used in the Bf 109F-4, gave a healthy boost in speed at all altitudes, allowing the Luftwaffe to keep pace with improvements in the Spitfire. For many German pilots the Bf 109F represented the peak of the fighter's development.

The next iteration of the Bf 109 was the G series, with both pressurized and unpressurized versions going into production. While using basically the same fuselage and wing shape as the Bf 109F, the G series benefited from a more powerful Daimler-Benz engine, the DB 605A. To boost the power output, Daimler-Benz redesigned the engine's cylinder block and rebored the cylinders to increase the displacement from 33.9 litres to 35.7 litres. The compression ratio increased to 7.3 for the port cylinder block and 7.5 for the starboard cylinder block. With other refinements the DB 605A produced 1,475hp. This gave the Bf 109G-2 – the first unpressurized version – a maximum speed of 398mph at 20,670ft. The pressurized Bf 109G-1 and the unpressurized Bf 109G-2 went into service in June 1942, followed by the Bf 109G-4 in November (only 50 examples of the pressurized Bf 109G-3 were built).

During this period of the war, the main problem with the Bf 109 was its comparatively limited armament. The Bf 109G-2 and G-4 retained the standard weaponry of the Bf 109F-4 series – two 7.92mm MG 17 machine guns in the nose, with 500 rounds per gun, and a 20mm MG 151 cannon with 200 rounds. While the

A wartime propaganda postcard showing a brand new Bf 109G-2 fresh from the Messerschmitt factory at Augsburg in the summer of 1942. The G-2 had all the aerodynamic refinements of the Bf 109F series, but replaced the DB 601N engine with the more powerful DB 605A. Despite the G-2 being 440lb heavier than the Bf 109F, the DB 605A gave it a faster maximum speed at high-altitude. (Author's Collection)

OPPOSITE

Oberleutnant Franz Schiess took over this Bf 109G-4/trop fitted with gondola-mounted MG 151 cannon when he was assigned as *Staffelkapitän* of 8./JG 53 on February 16, 1943. Despite flying from bases on Sicily, the aircraft retained the standard Luftwaffe desert camouflage scheme of RLM 78/79 with white spinner, underwing tips and fuselage band theater markings. It also had additional dark green in a splinter pattern applied to its upper wing surfaces. On joining 8./JG 53, Schiess had already claimed 37 Soviet, British and American aircraft shot down, including five Lightnings while flying with *Stab./JG 53*. "Black 1" was later destroyed in a ground collision after it had been passed on to another pilot in 8. *Staffel*.

Bf 109G-4/trop

29ft 7in.

8ft 2.5in.

32ft 6.5in.

The DB 605A that powered the Bf 109G-2, G-4 and many Bf 109G-6 aircraft. The engine featured a complete re-design of the cylinder block to obtain the maximum bore, increasing the capacity from 33.9 litres in the DB 601 to 35.7 litres, boosting take-off power to 1,475hp. A MG 151 20mm cannon fired through the hollow propeller shaft. (AIR 40/61, National Archives, London)

two rifle-caliber machine guns and single 20mm cannon were reasonably adequate for fighter-versus-fighter combat, the Messerschmitt was now having a hard time coping with the four-engined USAAF bombers starting to enter combat over Europe. After several encounters between Bf 109G-2s and G-4s and B-17 Flying Fortresses over Tunisia, in February 1943 the *Fliegerführer Tunis* reported that "Numerous cases in recent days of hits scored but no aircraft brought down show that existing gun armament is inadequate to shoot down four-engined bombers."

As an expedient, Messerschmitt fitted a gondola-mounted MG 151 20mm cannon, with 120 rounds per gun, under each wing of the Bf 109 as the *Rüstaztz* (Field Conversion Set) R6. This added significant fire power, but had a deleterious effect on the Bf 109's flying characteristics. A more permanent solution was to upgrade the aircraft's nose armament. For the pressurized Bf 109G-5 and the unpressurized Bf-109G-6, built in greater numbers than any other version, Messerschmitt replaced the two MG 17s with two more powerful 13mm MG 131 machine guns, each with 600 rounds, and later replaced the MG 151 20mm cannon with the Mk 108 30mm cannon.

With the G series, the weight of the Messerschmitt fighter had gone up by nearly 1,320lbs over the Bf 109E, with the Bf 109G-6 weighing 6,834lbs. The DB 605A engine was heavier than previous models and required some structural strengthening, which in turn meant a heavier undercarriage. Bulges to cover the larger MG 131 machine guns marred the sleek nose of the Bf 109F series. As a result, the Bf 109G-6 was slightly slower than the G-2 or G-4, and its handling qualities suffered due to the progressive increases in weight. The Bf 109's narrow track undercarriage had always been a challenge in take-offs and landings, and this became more so as younger, greener pilots transitioned to this powerful fighter. It is noteworthy that in the figure for Luftwaffe fighters written off between January and October 1942, nearly as many (presumably mostly Bf 109s) were written off due to causes other than enemy action as were lost in combat.

TECHNICAL
SPECIFICATIONS

P-38 LIGHTNING

P-38F

Lockheed began delivering the P-38F to the USAAF in March 1942. The F-model was fully combat capable. The nose compartment housed four Browning M2 0.50-cal. machine guns, with magazines holding 500 rounds per gun, and the Hispano M1 20mm cannon, with a magazine holding 150 rounds. Expended 0.50-cal. links and cartridges

P-38F-1 41-7582 was assigned to the 94th FS/1st FG in North Africa. The F-model Lightning was the first example of the Lockheed fighter to be produced in quantity, and it was also the first to see combat with German fighters over North Africa and Japanese fighters over New Guinea and Guadalcanal. This aircraft was lost in a crash in French Morocco on December 28, 1943 apparently while serving in an operational training unit. (2008-03-31_image_586_01, Peter M. Bowers Collection, MoF)

went out through chutes below the armament compartment, while 20mm links and shells were collected in a special compartment on the lower right hand side of the central nacelle.

The pilot was protected from frontal attack by a section of armor plate mounted on the aft bulkhead of the armament compartment and a bullet-proof glass windscreen. The pilot's seat had two pieces of armor plate on the bottom and in the back, and an additional piece of armor plate was mounted above and behind the seat. Armor plate or deflectors on the inboard sides of the turbosuperchargers protected the pilot against fragmentation of the supercharger blades.

The early model P-38s featured a large control wheel, with the top quarter open, instead of a control column. The four 0.50-cal. machine guns could be fired by pressing a button on the front of the control wheel, with a similar button for the 20mm cannon just behind. Due to the P-38's heavy weight, relatively small wing and small ailerons, rolling the aircraft required high control forces and forceful operation of the control wheel.

Each engine had its own separate fuel system, but they were interconnected so that fuel from any tank was available for either engine. The center section housed four fuel tanks, with the two main tanks holding 93 US gallons of, typically, 100 octane fuel, and two reserve tanks containing 60 US gallons. Pylons under the center section could carry two pressed steel drop tanks holding 150 US gallons of fuel (although often listed as 165 gallons). The pylons could also carry a 1,000lb bomb.

Lockheed built 526 P-38Fs. As production expanded, new F-models went to fighter groups re-equipping with the Lightning, replacing earlier P-38D/Es, P-40s and Republic P-43s that had been used to train pilots until sufficient Lightnings could be obtained.

P-38G

The P-38G was virtually indistinguishable from the preceding F-model. Armament was exactly the same, but the later P-38G-10 version had strengthened pylons under the center section that allowed the aircraft to carry larger 300-gallon pressed steel drop tanks or 2,000lb bombs. The -10 version could also carry triple-tube 4.5-in. rocket launchers mounted on either side of the fuselage. As with the P-38F, the G-model had the main canopy side panels reinforced with X-shaped frames and bracing for the upper section that was hinged to the rear. The P-38G also had the N9 gunsight in place of the N3B of earlier models.

The main difference between the F- and G-model Lightning was the change in engine. In the P-38G, Lockheed installed the improved Allison V-1710-51/55, which allowed higher settings for military and

The P-38G had an improved Allison V-1750 engine which gave higher military and maximum continuous power than the engines fitted in the F-model Lightning. Apart from some other minor modifications, the two models were similar, however. The pilot of this aircraft, 2Lt Lawrence P. Liebers (left), shown here talking to his crew chief, TSgt Roswell Harding, claimed five Italian C.202 and C.205 fighters and two German Fw 190s shot down while flying with the 96th FS/14th FG in 1943. (3A-27869, Record Group 342FH, NARA)

maximum continuous power over the P-38F. Where the latter had been restricted to 1,240hp for take-off, 1,325hp for military power at 15,000ft and 1,000hp for maximum continuous power at 27,000ft, the P-38G had 1,425hp for military power and 1,100hp for maximum continuous power at 24,000ft.

The P-38G weighed around 100lbs less than the P-38F, coming in at 15,800lbs with maximum internal fuel and 17,800lbs with maximum internal fuel and two 150-gallon drop tanks. With slightly lower weight and a bit more power, the P-38G had a faster rate of climb at altitude than the F-model. It was the same up to 10,000ft, but at 15,000ft, the G-model could climb at 1,700ft per minute, and at 1,000ft per minute at 25,000ft, compared to 1,500ft and 900ft per minute in the P-38F.

P-38F/G LIGHTNING NOSE GUNS

With the P-38E, the USAAF standardized the Lightning's armament in all future models as one Hispano M1 20mm cannon and four Browning M2 0.50-cal. machine guns. As with the Bf 109, locating all the armament in the Lightning's nose was close to ideal, for the direction of fire was directly in the pilot's line of sight, with no convergence. The 0.50-cal. M2 machine gun fired at a rate of 600 to 850 rounds per minute, whilst the M1 20mm cannon could expend 600 to 700 rounds per minute. A one-second burst from a P-38 weighed 7.8lbs, compared to the armament in a Bf 109G-2/4, which put out 4.1lbs. The Lightning's guns were aligned to fire in a pattern 20-in. in diameter.

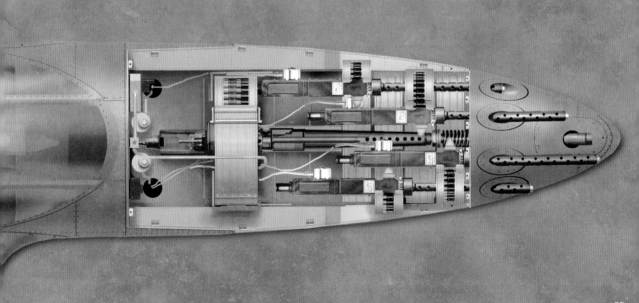

Messerschmitt began manufacturing the Bf 109G-2 in the spring of 1942, with the G-2/trop began replacing the Bf 109F/trop in the *Jagdgruppen* assigned to the Mediterranean from September 1942. By the time of the invasion of North Africa on November 8, 1942, II./JG 51 and JG 53 – the first Luftwaffe units to confront the P-38s – were completely equipped with the Bf 109G-2/trop. This early-build G-2/trop from 4./JG 53 is having its guns boresighted at Bir El Abd, in Egypt, shortly after its arrival in North Africa in September 1942. (Tony Holmes Collection)

At altitude, the P-38G was also slightly faster, with a top speed of 400mph at 25,000ft compared to 395mph in the P-38F.

Deliveries of the P-38G began in August 1942, and continued until March 1943.

Bf 109G

Bf 109G-1

The Bf 109G-1 was the first model of the G series to enter production, with the first examples sent to 1. and 11./JG 2 in June 1942 to form special high-altitude *staffeln* (squadrons). The G-1 had a pressurised cockpit, with the canopy constructed of welded framing. The small triangular pane at the front of the canopy – a recognition feature of the Bf 109F series – was omitted. The G-1 and subsequent G-models had two small air scoops fitted on both sides of the cowling to cool the oil tank and spark plugs. The armor plate behind the pilot's head, which had been angled in previous models, was squared off to seal the rear of the canopy. A built-in armored glass windscreen replaced the external armored windscreen on the Bf 109F series. The G-1 retained the same armament as the F series – two MG 17 7.92mm machine guns and a single MG 151 20mm cannon. The tailwheel was fixed, with the recessed area blanked off.

Bf 109G-2

Production of the Bf 109G-2 began at the same time as the Bf 109G-1 at the Erla and Messerschmitt Regensburg factories, and later the Wiener Neustädter Flugzeugwerke, which continued to build the G-2 until February 1943. Total production amounted to some 1,586 G-2s. Like the Bf 109G-1, the G-2 featured the improved DB 605A engine generating 1,475hp. The major difference with the G-1 was the deletion of the fittings for pressurization. The G-2 returned to the angled head armor behind the pilot, attached to the cockpit canopy, and featured the built-in armored windscreen ahead of the pilot. Several *Rüstätze* sets could be fitted to the G-2, including the R1, R2 and R4 incorporating bomb racks, the R3 accommodating a 300-litre drop tank and the R6 set for the two underwing gondolas holding the MG 151 15mm or 20mm cannon. The tropical version of the Bf 109G-2, designated the G-2/trop, featured a sand filter attached to the supercharger intake on the port side of the fuselage,

reinforced tires and a desert survival kit placed in the rear fuselage that contained a radio, water, food and a Kar 98K rifle. Two small brackets attached to the fuselage below the cockpit held a sun umbrella to protect pilots on readiness from the intense heat in the Mediterranean and North Africa.

Bf 109G-4

The Bf 109G-4 began reaching *Jagdgruppen* in November 1942. Like the Bf 109G-2 before it, the G-4 served on every front and with almost all *Jagdgruppen*. There were several external differences between the G-4 and the G-2. As the weight of the Bf 109 was steadily increasing, the G-4 had larger mainwheels and tailwheel. The 25.6-in. x 5.9-in. wheels of the Bf 109F and G-2 models were replaced with 26-in. x 6.3-in. mainwheels, which were mounted at a more vertical angle. This required teardrop-shaped fairings to be installed in the upper wings – the first of the bulges that would earn the later G series the nickname of *Beule* (bump). A larger 13.8-in. x 5.3-in. tailwheel replaced the earlier 11.4-in. x 4.3-in. version. The larger tailwheel could not be retracted into the fuselage, so the retraction mechanism was simply disconnected. The G-4 model replaced the FuG VIIa radio in the G-2 with a VHF FuG 16Z radio. The Bf 109G-4/trop (the version encountered most often by P-38 units over North Africa, Sicily and Italy) had the same modifications as the Bf 109G-2/trop. The G-4 could also take the same *Rüstätze* sets as the G-2. The *Jagdgruppen* assigned to *Luftflotte* 2 in the Mediterranean during late 1942 and early 1943 were equipped with both the Bf 109G-2 and the Bf 109G-4, until the Bf 109G-6 began arriving in the spring and summer of 1943.

Bf 109G-6

The Bf 109G-6 was the final Bf 109 variant that USAAF P-38 Lightning pilots met in combat during 1943. The main difference with the earlier G-4 was the change in armament from the 7.92mm MG 17 machine guns to the heavier 13mm MG 131 machine guns with 300 rounds per weapon. As the chutes for spent cartridges from the MG 131s would not fit under the standard Bf 109 cowling, two circular fairings had to be added to each side of the nose, altering the profile. Bf 109G-6s operating from Sicily and Italy are frequently pictured with the *Rüstätze* R6 set of underwing

This Bf 109G-4/trop, complete with its distinctive sand filter attached to the supercharger intake immediately to the left of the pilot, of 6./JG 51 was photographed between missions at an airfield on Sicily or southern Italy in the summer of 1943. II./JG 51 took delivery of its first Bf 109G-4s in February 1943 to supplement Bf 109G-2s that had been assigned to the unit in October 1942. During March–April 1943, the *Gruppe* flew the Bf 109G-4 alongside its older G-2s and newly arrived Bf 109G-6s. By the end of May, the G-6 had completely replaced the Bf 109G-4/trop in II./JG 51. JG 53 also flew the Bf 109G-4/trop from January to April 1943, although a few lingered on until July. (B.A.1011-468-1414-15)

Bf 109G-2/4 MACHINE GUNS

The Bf 109G-2/4 retained the two Rheinmetall MG 17 7.92mm machine guns in the nose that had been the standard armament of all previous Bf 109 models. Like the Bf 109F series, the ammunition load in the Bf 109G-2/4 was reduced from 1,000 to 500 rounds per gun. A typical loading was 50 percent armor-piercing, 40 percent armor-piercing incendiary and ten percent high-explosive incendiary rounds. The MG 17 had a rate of fire of 1,200 rounds per minute, but the weight of the 7.92mm cartridge was only a quarter of the weight of the American 0.50-cal. round.

Bf 109G-2/4 CANNON

With the Mauser MG 151 15mm cannon having been deemed inadequate, the Bf 109G-2/4 was equipped with the engine-mounted MG 151/20 20mm weapon initially introduced in the Bf 109F-4. Its magazine held 200 rounds of ammunition, typically with a mix of high explosive incendiary, armor-piercing or armor-piercing high explosive rounds firing at a rate of 700 rounds per minute. While adequate for fighter-versus-fighter combat, the Bf 109G-2/4's armament proved ineffective against USAAF B-17 and B-24 bombers. The nose armament could be augmented with two underwing MG 151/20 20mm cannon as the *Rüstsätze* R6 field modification kit, but this had a deleterious effect on the aircraft's handling qualities.

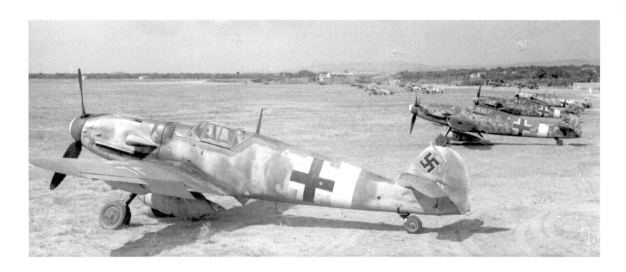

MG 151 cannon gondolas for attacking American heavy bombers. The Bf 109G-6 could also carry the 21cm *Bord-Rakete* weapon, a tube-mounted *Wurfgranate 42* mortar shell that was fired at bombers. However, the drag these weapons produced, with one mounted under each wing, had a severe effect on the Bf 109G-6's maneuverability. The G-6 had the larger mainwheels and fixed tailwheel of the G-4. The Bf 109G-2, G-4 and early-production G-6 models used the Revi C 12/C and C 12/D gunsights, with the latter being calibrated for bombing and fixed gunnery.

P-38F and Bf 109G-2 Comparison Specifications

	P-38F	Bf 109G-2
Powerplant	2 x 1,325hp Allison V-1710-49/53	1,475hp Daimler-Benz DB 605A
Dimensions		
Span	52ft 0in.	32ft 6.5in.
Length	37ft 10in.	29ft 7in.
Height	12ft 10in.	8ft 2.5in.
Wing area	327.5 sq. ft	174.37 sq. ft
Weights		
Empty	12,200lbs	4,968lbs
Loaded	17,800lbs	6,834lbs
Wing loading	54.3lb/sq. ft	39.19lb/sq. ft
Performance		
Max speed	395mph at 25,000ft	398mph at 20,670ft
Range	960 miles	528 miles
Climb	20,000ft in 6 min.	19,685ft in 3.2 min
Service ceiling	39,000ft	39,370ft
Armament	4 x 0.50-cal. Browning M2s 1 x 20mm Hispano M1	2 x 7.92mm MG 17s 1 x 20mm MG 151

THE STRATEGIC SITUATION

At the Arcadia Conference, held in Washington, D.C. from December 21, 1941 to January 14, 1942, President Franklin D. Roosevelt, Prime Minister Winston Churchill and the combined American and British Chiefs of Staff met to plan out Allied strategy for the war against Germany, Italy and Japan. At previous meetings it had already been decided that in the event of America's entry into the war, the overall strategy would be to defeat Germany first. The question was where and how to begin.

The American preference was for a direct assault on Europe as early as possible. The British had a more realistic view of Allied capabilities, and argued that a cross-Channel invasion in 1942 and possibly even in 1943 was premature. Churchill believed that the Allies should begin by tightening the ring around Germany, first securing the North African coast and using this as a base for knocking Italy out of the war. Removing Axis forces from North Africa would eliminate any threat to the oil supplies in the Middle East, while defeating Italy would free up the sea lines of communication through the Mediterranean, greatly easing constraints on Allied shipping.

While the US Army opposed what it saw as a diversion away from the main thrust against Germany, Roosevelt remained interested in Churchill's proposal. With Japan rampaging through the Pacific and Southeast Asia, the need to build up Allied defenses against further Japanese advances and protect Australia took precedent over allocating troops and shipping to Europe. An assault on North Africa had to be postponed.

Having declared war on America on December 11, 1941, Adolf Hitler now found Germany in conflict with all the great powers of the world, and his political and strategic options diminishing. While Hitler's focus remained on the defeat of the Soviet Union, he and the Wehrmacht could not ignore the risk of American and British moves against German-occupied Europe, particularly attacks on the periphery, from where the Allies could launch air and ground offensives on the European mainland.

There were three areas that were under threat: Vichy French Morocco, linked with an advance from Egypt to capture all of North Africa; an advance from the Middle East to support the USSR; and developing facilities in England as a base for air and ground campaigns against Europe. Maintaining Axis control over North Africa and the Mediterranean was deemed essential, as their loss would open up Europe to an invasion from the south. The German high command was increasingly aware that it did not have the forces necessary to protect all the areas under threat and maintain the offensive against the Soviet Union.

Over the summer of 1942, American and British leadership renewed discussions on invading North Africa. The strategic situation had changed. In Europe, Hitler had launched a massive offensive in the USSR aimed at capturing the oil fields in the Caucasus, while the German *Afrika Korps* was pushing British forces back toward Egypt. A landing in North Africa, it was hoped, would draw German air and ground forces away from the Soviet Union and threaten the German advance toward Egypt. Landings in North Africa now seemed the best option for confronting the Axis in 1942.

Designated Operation *Torch*, the landings were scheduled for the fall, with American forces simultaneously attacking Casablanca, on the Atlantic coast of Vichy French Morocco, and Oran, in Vichy French Algeria, with a combined American and British force also landing at Algiers. The objective of *Torch* was to secure Vichy French Morocco, Algeria and Tunisia, and bring about the defeat of Axis forces in the Western Desert.

To support the invasion, the USAAF activated the Twelfth Air Force, with an initial combat force of two heavy bomber groups, three medium bomber groups, a light bomber group, two P-38 groups (1st and 14th FGs) and two Spitfire groups. The heavy bombers and the fighter groups were to be drawn from the Eighth Air Force in England, augmented by forces from the US. More units would join the Twelfth Air Force in the months following the landings in North Africa on November 8, 1942, including a third P-38 group (82nd FG) and two more heavy and two medium bomber groups. At the time of the landings, the combined strength

The Twelfth Air Force initially had two heavy bombardment groups, the 97th and the 301st, equipped with B-17s. In early 1943 two more groups, the 2nd and the 99th, arrived in North Africa. Together with the B-24s of the Ninth Air Force, they undertook a campaign of aerial interdiction, with RAF Wellington bombers attacking by night. B-17F Flying Fortress 41-24618 *Lil Jo* was assigned to the 352nd BS/ 301st BG. Later transfered to the 2nd BG, it was shot down by enemy fighters and Flak during a raid on Steyr, in Austria, on February 24, 1944. (Author's Collection)

of USAAF and RAF units in Eastern Air Command amounted to around 1,700 aircraft.

For the Luftwaffe, the landings in North Africa represented one more drain on an already over-extended force. At the end of October the British Eighth Army in Egypt successfully engaged the *Afrika Korps* during the pivotal Second Battle of El Alamein, forcing the German and Italian armies into retreat. On November 8 came the landings in North Africa, and 11 days later the Red Army launched a massive offensive that would

Pilots from II./JG 53 discuss the combat of March 22, 1943 with their commanding officer, Hauptmann Gerhard Michalski, at La Marsa, in Tunisia. Closest to the camera, from left to right, are Unteroffizier Otto Russ, who claimed a P-38 destroyed that day, Hauptmann Willi Krauss, Oberleutnant Fritz Dinger (his Bf 109G-4 can be seen behind him), Hauptmann Gerhard Michalski and Leutnant Wolfgang Dreifke, both of whom also claimed a P-38, and Feldwebel Friedrich Steinmüller. Russ, Dinger, Michalski and Steinmüller would be credited with a total of 13 Lightnings between them while serving with II./JG 53. (B.A. Bild 1011-420-2030-14A)

eventually surround the German 6th Army at Stalingrad. The Allied air offensive against German-occupied Europe was expanding by both day and night. The Luftwaffe was now on the defensive, and it could only fill gaps in one front by creating gaps in another. Toward the end of 1942, the Luftwaffe began stripping units from the Eastern Front to send to the Mediterranean, to Western Europe and to the Reich.

With a shorter line of communications than that of the Allies, the Axis forces rushed replacements of men, equipment and aircraft to Tunisia, halting the Allied drive at the border with Algeria. December brought heavy rain, and with a lack of resources for the Allied armies and air forces in-theater, a stalemate developed that lasted until the spring.

The battle for Tunisia turned into a battle of logistics. *Luftflotte* 2, controlling Luftwaffe units in the Mediterranean, received reinforcements of bombers and fighters. By December there were nine day fighter *Gruppen* assigned to the Mediterranean, comprising II./JG 51, I., II. and III./JG 53 and II./JG 2 operating over Tunisia and Sicily, I., II. and III./JG 77 supporting the retreating *Afrika Korps* in Libya and III./JG 27 in Greece and Crete – II./JG 51 and II./JG 77 had been withdrawn from the Eastern Front. Operating from all-weather airfields in Tunisia and Sicily, the Luftwaffe successfully contested Allied attempts to establish air superiority over Tunisia and, for a few months, retained the initiative in the air.

The Twelfth Air Force, in contrast, lacked all-weather airfields and was suffering from an acute shortage of supplies, replacement pilots, aircraft and groundcrew. Despite these limitations, and the poor weather, the Twelfth initiated a campaign of aerial interdiction that grew in intensity. The heavy and medium bomber groups, with P-38 escorts, carried out attacks on Axis airfields, docks and harbor facilities, shipping, and marshaling yards in Tunisia, Sardinia, Sicily and Italy. In February, the Allied air forces underwent a reorganization that created the MAAF. USAAF and RAF units supporting the drive to Tunisia now came under Northwest African Air Force control, falling into strategic, tactical and coastal commands.

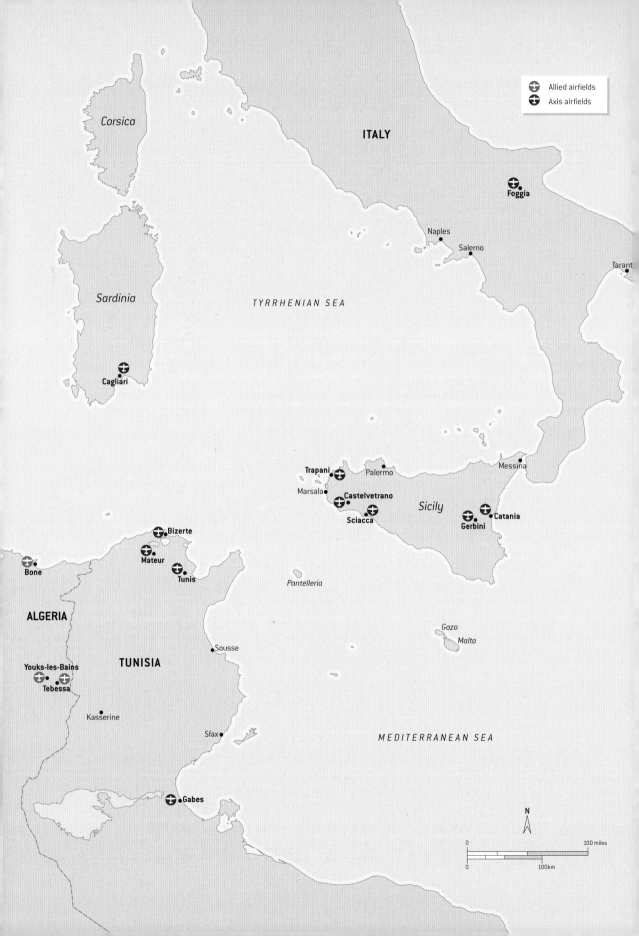

Allied airfields
Axis airfields

Corsica

ITALY

Foggia

Naples
Salerno

Taranto

Sardinia

TYRRHENIAN SEA

Cagliari

Palermo

Messina

Trapani
Marsala
Castelvetrano
Sciacca
Gerbini
Catania

Sicily

Bizerte
Mateur
Tunis

Bone

ALGERIA

Pantelleria

Gozo
Malta

Youks-les-Bains
Tebessa

TUNISIA

Sousse

Kasserine

Sfax

MEDITERRANEAN SEA

Gabes

N

0   100 miles

0   100km

By the end of February 1943 the tide had begun to turn in favor of the Allies. The Luftwaffe had become increasingly ineffective in interdicting the flow of Allied supplies to North Africa, enabling American and British forces to overcome their earlier logistical difficulties. The Allies now had 2,769 aircraft available against 837 for the Luftwaffe and around 100 for the Regia Aeronautica. Two new B-17 groups and a B-25 and a B-26 group joined the NASAF and a third P-38 group returned to combat, allowing the aerial interdiction campaign to expand in reach and effort, with the USAAF bombing by day and the RAF by night. During January 1943 American heavy bombers of the Twelfth and Ninth (based in Egypt) Air Forces had dropped 1,354 tons of bombs. In April the total reached 2,777 tons, and in May 4,305 tons. The cumulative effect of the destruction of harbor facilities, shipping losses and transport aircraft shot down severely disrupted the flow of supplies to Axis forces in Tunisia.

By the end of March, Luftwaffe units in Tunisia had lost air superiority to the Allies. Advancing through Libya, the British Eighth Army broke through the Mareth Line and advanced into Tunisia. Combined offensives in March and April pushed the Axis further and further back into Tunisia until all German and Italian forces in North Africa surrendered on May 13, 1943.

The loss of Tunisia was a debacle for the Wehrmacht and the Luftwaffe, with the Allies capturing around 270,000 Axis soldiers. Between November 1942 and May 1943, the Luftwaffe lost 2,422 aircraft in-theater, including 633 aircraft captured on the ground when Tunisia fell. The *Jagdgruppen* suffered losses of 888 fighters in the air and on the ground, as well as having to leave behind vital equipment in North Africa. Many of the Bf 109 units left Tunisia in early May, with one and sometimes two groundcrew stuffed in the rear fuselage of a Bf 109 for the flight to airfields in Sicily. Once back to bases in Sicily, Italy and Sardinia, the battered *Jagdgruppen* received reinforcements of pilots and aircraft, with the number of available fighters increasing from 190 in May to 450 in July.

At the Casablanca Conference in January 1943, the Allies decided that Sicily would be the next target for invasion after the fall of Tunisia. Codenamed Operation *Husky*, the capture of Sicily would give the Allies command over the Mediterranean and provide a base for an invasion of Italy. An advance up the Italian peninsula would likely tie down German forces that could be used on the Eastern Front or to defend against a cross-Channel invasion, while capturing the airfields around Foggia, in southern Italy, would provide bases for USAAF heavy bombers in an expanded combined bomber offensive, also approved at the Casablanca Conference.

There was little the Luftwaffe could do to counter an Allied invasion force, wherever the Allies decided to land. On 10 July 1943, the date of the invasion of Sicily, *Luftflotte* 2 had nine Bf 109 *Gruppen* of day fighters (IV./JG 3, II./JG 27, II./JG 51, I., II. and III./JG 53 and I., II. and III./JG 77) available based in Sicily, Sardinia and southern Italy, with 165 operational aircraft between them. There were also three fighter-bomber and two ground-attack *Gruppen*, with 79 operational Fw 190 fighters, in-theater.

In contrast, for the invasion the MAAF assembled 23 squadrons of RAF Kittyhawks and USAAF P-40s, 18 squadrons of RAF and USAAF Spitfires, six squadrons of USAAF A-36 dive-bombers and nine squadrons of P-38s, all of which were assigned

OPPOSITE

This map shows the key locations of Luftwaffe Bf 109 and USAAF P-38 airfields during the fighting in North Africa in the wake of the Operation *Torch* landings on November 10, 1942. All Bf 109 *Gruppen* were pulled back to Sicily and Sardinia just prior to the fall of Tunisia on May 13, 1943.

to the NASAF. All told, the MAAF mustered 3,462 combat aircraft, of which 2,510 were operational, compared to 932 aircraft of all types in *Luftflotte* 2, with 563 operational, and 930 in the Regia Aeronautica, with 449 operational.

In the weeks leading up to the invasion of Sicily, NASAF B-17 Flying Fortresses and Ninth Air Force B-24 Liberators hammered Luftwaffe airfields on Sicily and Sardinia and in Italy, and continued their attacks on key port facilities. To *Reichsmarschall* Hermann Göring's wrath, the *Jagdgruppen* could do little against the massed American bomber formations and their P-38 escorts. American losses of heavy and medium bombers to enemy aircraft in the Mediterranean amounted to six aircraft in June and 26 in July. During July and August the USAAF heavy bombers dropped 11,930 tons of bombs on targets in the Mediterranean, while medium and light bombers expended an additional 11,628 tons. Although there were isolated incidents where the *Jagdgruppen* did inflict losses on Allied aircraft, the air onslaught was relentless and inexorable.

On July 10, the date of the invasion of Sicily, the Luftwaffe and the Regia Aeronautica flew 511 sorties over the island. Five days later, they managed just 161 sorties. On August 11 the Germans began to evacuate Sicily and on the 17th American and British forces linked up in Messina, establishing full control over the island. Less than a month later, American and British divisions landed on the Italian mainland. On September 8, 1943, a day before the landings at Salerno, the Italian government surrendered to the Allies.

The Luftwaffe had suffered another significant and costly defeat. During the month of July, 711 German aircraft were lost over Sicily, with a further 321 shot down or destroyed on the ground in southern Italy as the Allies continued attacks. Following the invasion of Italy, the Luftwaffe pulled several *Jagdgruppen* back to Germany to refit in preparation for the defense of the Reich and battles on the Eastern Front. As the months went by, the Luftwaffe withdrew more and more aircraft from the Mediterranean. By July 1944, the Luftwaffe had only 300 frontline aircraft in the area.

The nature of the air war changed. As Allied armies continued their slow progress up through Italy, with support from USAAF and RAF tactical air forces, the tactical fighters would battle the few German fighters remaining in-theater. The Fifteenth Air Force, activated in November 1943, became part of the strategic air campaign against Germany, flying missions into central Europe with escorts of long-range P-38, P-47 and P-51 fighters. Large-scale aerial battles with the Luftwaffe would now take place over Austria, southern Germany and central European cities, rather than over Italy.

A P-38F from the 94th FS/1st FG returns to an airfield in Algeria following another escort mission to Sicily. The Lightning's long range enabled the P-38s to escort American bombers to any target in Sardinia, Sicily and southern Italy as far as Rome. With cover all the way to and from the target, the bombers could carry out a successful aerial interdiction campaign without suffering heavy losses to Axis fighters. (3A-28555, RG 342FH, NARA)

THE COMBATANTS

USAAF PILOT TRAINING

Many of the pilots who flew P-38 Lightnings over North Africa, Sicily and Italy completed their flying training during 1941–42 – a period of exponential growth for the USAAF. In 1939, the USAAC had established a plan to expand to 24 groups and train 1,200 pilots a year. In March 1940 a revised plan went into effect calling for 41 groups and 7,000 pilots a year. After the fall of France in June 1940, this plan, too, was revised upward to 54 groups and 12,000 pilots a year. It lasted less than a year. As American rearmament accelerated, in March 1941 the USAAC established a new plan calling for 84 groups and the training of 30,000 pilots a year, an expansion of 3,000 percent over the pre-war training effort.

In 1939, the USAAC produced just 982 graduates of advanced flying schools. During 1940, 1,786 pilots graduated from advanced flying training schools. This number jumped to 7,244 in 1941 and 24,948 in 1942. This rate of growth put an immense strain on the USAAC/USAAF training effort.

To increase the flow of pilots, the USAAC decided to change the structure of Primary training. It determined that it would be too costly and take too much time to build the many primary flying schools and airfields that would be needed for expansion. Instead, the USAAC and later the USAAF contracted with private flying schools to provide facilities and instructors to conduct Primary training of aviation cadets. By early 1940, nine contract schools were in operation – ultimately, 41 schools across the US undertook primary training.

The government provided Primary training aircraft and assigned USAAC/USAAF officers to oversee the training program and the civilian instructors. These officers served as check pilots for both instructors and students, with the latter being assessed at the completion of their Primary training. By the time of the attack on Pearl Harbor on December 7, 1941, the length of the Primary training course had been cut from 12 to ten weeks, and then shortened again to nine weeks.

Prior to America's entry into the war, the USAAC drew pilot candidates primarily from university students who had completed at least two years of college courses or an equivalent. Some of those who enlisted in the USAAC during 1940–41 were graduates of the Civilian Pilot Training Program, where they had received basic flying instruction in small aircraft.

The objective of Primary training was to teach basic flying skills. The student pilot learned to safely take off and land an aircraft and execute basic flight manoeuvers such as stalls, spins, chandelles and figure eights. In the Primary phase, the student accumulated 60 flying hours and spent some 140 hours in classes. Although civilians ran the schools and served as instructors, the students were subject to military discipline and underwent military drills. There was no standard Primary trainer, with different schools using different aircraft – primarily Stearman PT-13 and PT-17 biplanes and Fairchild PT-19 and Ryan PT-20, PT-21 and PT-22 monoplanes. The washout rate in Primary training was around 30 percent. Those who successfully passed the Primary course moved on to Basic training, where their instructors were all military pilots and the atmosphere and emphasis was decidedly more military.

In the early years of USAAF expansion, the focus in Basic training was on learning to fly with precision. The student flew more advanced maneuvers and started formation flying, moving on to night flying, instrument flying and basic navigation by day and by night in the Vultee BT-13 fixed-gear monoplane. By the end of the Basic course, a student would have accumulated around 70 hours of flying, with more time spent in the classroom studying aeronautical subjects and hours of military drill. In Basic school, students began training in instrument flying and would undertake longer cross-country flights, often in formation. At the end of the Basic training phase, students were assigned to Advanced training in either single-engined aircraft, leading to training as a fighter pilot, or twin-engined aircraft, which meant becoming a bomber or transport pilot.

During 1940–41, the USAAC's pilot training program expanded exponentially. Many of the men who flew P-38s in North Africa completed their training during 1941 and early 1942. The North American AT-6, multiple examples of which are shown here in July 1941, became the standard trainer in the Advanced training stage for pilots selected for single-engined fighters. (3B-24067, RG 342FH, NARA)

In the single-engined Advanced training course, the student pilot flew the more powerful North American AT-6 trainer. The Advanced course also lasted nine weeks, with the first days spent transitioning to the AT-6, after which students concentrated on more formation work, navigation (with more demanding cross-country flights), instrument flying and aerobatics. At some schools toward the end of the course, student pilots began working on aerial and ground gunnery and basic combat maneuvers. By the end of the Advanced course, a student had moved

in careful stages to aircraft of greater power and complexity to the point where, in the final weeks of training, he would be flying operational fighters like the Curtiss P-36 or P-40. Graduation brought the transition to frontline combat aircraft. With some fighters, the transition from the AT-6 was a bit of a jump. With the P-38, in the early months of the war, it was more of a leap.

Helping young pilots fresh out of Advanced training transition to the P-38, considered at the time to be a "hot" fighter, presented the USAAF with a challenge. It had decided that prospective Lightning pilots should be drawn from graduates of the Advanced single-engined training program, as these men had received some tuition in fighter tactics and aerial gunnery. But learning to fly an aircraft of far greater power than an AT-6, with two engines and two of everything else, and particularly learning how to fly a twin-engined fighter on a single engine, meant a would-be P-38 pilot really needed time at the controls of a twin-engined aircraft before being strapped into the cockpit of a Lightning. It took some time for USAAF Training Command to organize a specific transition training program for P-38 pilots. Until this emerged later in 1942, transition training for the Lightning was something of a catch-as-catch-can.

Initially, the P-38 was viewed with scepticism among some single-seat fighter pilots. The belief that loss of an engine on take-off could cause a fatal spin, that bailing out was problematic and that the aircraft had problems diving from high altitude caused some pilots to question the wisdom of converting to the Lightning. When pilots of the 14th PG learned in February 1942 that the group was to convert from the P-40 and P-43 to the P-38, a number requested transfers to bomber units. For many others, the challenge of taking on the USAAF's newest and best performing fighter was one that they had to take on. At the time, however, there were not enough P-38s to equip the several fighter groups forming on the new fighter, nor enough twin-engined trainers that could be spared from training future bomber pilots. Fighter groups and squadrons did the best they could with what they could get their hands on.

In his memoir *Happy Jack's Go Buggy*, Jack Ilfrey, who flew the P-38 in combat over North Africa and Europe, describes his first encounter with the aircraft, which he held in awe. Graduating from Advanced training in December 1941, Ilfrey was assigned to the famous 94th PS/1st PG and commenced flying the P-38 without any other training:

In those days, we first read the flight manual over, several times. We walked around

The rush to equip newly-formed P-38 groups took precedence over providing Lightnings for transition training. In the early months, many pilots had to fly whatever twin-engined aircraft was available. Some in the 14th FG gained twin-engined experience flying Lockheed C-36 transports. (3B-26964, RG 342FH, NARA)

and around the P-38 with the flight leader. We were taught the proper procedures and fired up the engines. Practiced taxiing until we got the gallop out of it. Then we were ready for our first take off. No "piggy-backs" in those days. It was the biggest thrill of my then young life. If you got it back on the ground, you were then a qualified P-38 pilot. Some didn't.

As the program for transitioning single-engined pilots to twin-engined fighters became more structured, trainees received five to ten hours of instruction on the Curtiss AT-9 before moving on to the Lockheed P-322. (3B-24199, RG 342FH, NARA)

The 14th PG acquired a Lockheed C-36 transport (a military version of the Lockheed 12 Electra) to give pilots some experience in handling two engines. They would practice taxiing the C-36 around the airfield and would then get around two hours of flying time before starting their transition to the P-38. Later on in the year the USAAF set up a program that would give students in Advanced training classes flights in the Curtiss AT-9 trainer or an equivalent twin-engined aircraft like the Beech AT-7 or AT-10. Pilots who completed their Advanced training from early 1943 onwards fared better, with more systematic training. Shortly before graduation, the students would be checked out in the AT-9, then go on to ground school to learn the P-38's systems. After several hours in the cockpit studying the instruments and controls, they would be given a ride in a "piggy-back" P-38 with the radios removed to allow for a passenger to sit behind the pilot.

After going solo in the Lightning and accumulating ten hours of flying, the pilots would go on to an Operational Training Unit (OTU) to learn how to fly a P-38 in combat. Pilots destined for the Lightning groups with the Twelfth Air Force would also spend time at a special OTU it had set up in North Africa, where tour-expired pilots instructed the new aviators in the latest combat tactics. Some of the first replacement pilots to arrive in North Africa in early 1943, however, had just 35–40 hours in the P-38, and many even less. After the USAAF instituted more specialized training programs, new pilots would arrive with double that amount of P-38 time.

LUFTWAFFE PILOT TRAINING

By the start of World War II on September 3, 1939, the Luftwaffe had established a flying training program that was equal in quality to any other European air arm. From the date of its official inception in March 1935, the Luftwaffe built up a training organization and developed programs for would-be pilots, aircrew and technical staff. As with most air forces, the Luftwaffe focused on building flying skills through a step by step progression to the point where a student pilot could become a fully capable combat flyer. The pilot training program remained basically the same up to 1942, when reversals in the war led to it being progressively shortened. The vast majority of the Bf 109 pilots who made multiple claims for

P-38s in the fighting over North Africa, Sicily and Italy had undertaken their training during the 1938–41 period, when the program was at its most effective.

In the Luftwaffe, pilots and aircrew were all volunteers. It selected recruits from the civilian population and from officers, NCOs and enlisted personnel in the Wehrmacht and Kriegsmarine (Navy). Entry into the Luftwaffe began with six months of military training at a *FliegerErsatzabteilung* (Aviator Replacement Department) using the same program as the Heer (Army) and the Kriegsmarine. The goal of the program was to instil in the Luftwaffe recruits the same military and disciplinary principles, creating a bond with the other services. The program taught basic military skills, covering physical training, military drill, familiarity with standard small arms and small-scale field exercises at platoon and company level. This program was later reduced to three months.

After completing their basic military training, recruits joined a *Flieger-Ausbildungsregiment* (Aviator Training Regiment) which had two components – a *Flieger-Ausbildunggruppe* (Aviator Training Regiment) and an associated *Flugzeugführerschule* (Pilot School) A/B. At the former, recruits spent two months studying aeronautics and were subject to careful examination for classification as pilots, observers or other positions. Recruits for pilot training were selected based on evaluations of their character, military ability, performance during training and testing, professions and interests and inclinations. If successful in being selected for pilot training, non-officers became part of a *Flug-Anwärterkompanie* (Flight Candidate Company), while officer candidates went to a *Luftkriegsschule* (Air Warfare School), where in addition to flying training they studied military tactics, air law and troop duty.

The goal of every pilot trainee at the A/B schools was to qualify for the *Luftwaffeflugzeugführerschein* (Luftwaffe Pilot's License), which allowed the holder to fly military aircraft. A secondary, but important goal of the A/B schools was to accurately evaluate a trainee's abilities in order to ascertain his suitability for advanced training programs. The schools were divided into an A phase and a B phase, corresponding to the weight, horsepower and complexity of the aircraft used in training.

To help pilots transition to the P-38, the USAAF took over the British contract for the Model 322 Lightning I, which lacked turbosuperchargers or counter rotating propellers – both were rejected by the RAF. Designated the P-322, the Lightning I had poor performance at altitude, but it gave new pilots valuable experience of flying a P-38. (15_001437, SDASM)

The A1 phase was the student pilot's introduction to flying, beginning with dual instruction in general handling of an aircraft. In the A1 phase, a student would fly the Focke-Wulf Fw 44 Stieglitz and Bücker Bü 133 biplanes and the Klemm Kl 35 and Bücker Bü 181 monoplanes. Students learned how to take off and land and perform basic maneuvers leading to solo flight. In the A2 phase the student would move on to slightly more powerful aircraft, continuing with the Fw 44 but also training in the Heinkel He 72, Arado Ar 66 and Bücker Bü 131 and Bü 181 monoplanes, and adding cross-country flights and formation flying to his skills.

The Focke-Wulf Fw 56 Stösser, shown here in a pre-war propaganda postcard, was used as an advanced trainer in fighter schools, introducing young pilots to a more powerful aircraft. The Fw 56, which was fitted with one or two MG 17 machine guns for gunnery training, had a maximum speed of 173mph. By the time production ended in 1940, Focke-Wulf had built nearly 1,000 Fw 56s. (Author's Collection)

During the B phase the student continued practicing maneuvers learned in the A phase, but in more powerful aircraft such as the Gotha Go 145, Junkers W34, Arado Ar 96 and Messerschmitt Bf 108. This phase added instrument and night flying, aerobatic flying and learning how to control an aircraft in emergency situations to the syllabus. By the end of the course a student pilot would have accumulated up to 150 hours of flying time, qualified for the *Luftwaffeflugzeugführerschein* (Air Force Pilot's License) and been awarded his pilot's badge.

Future fighter pilots were carefully selected from the graduates of the A/B schools based on their flying ability, physical fitness, personality and results of psychological testing. If selected, graduates began with initial fighter training at a *Jagdfliegervorschulen* (Fighter Pilot Pre-school), before moving on to one of several *Jagdfliegerschule* (Fighter Pilot School), where they received some four months of specialized training in fighter tactics and gunnery. Training began with conversion to advanced trainers, initially the Arado Ar 76 and the Focke-Wulf Fw 56 Stösser.

Once fully capable of flying these types, thorough training in formation flying was the next stage. Students began with the two-man *Rotte* (Pack) formation, before moving on to the four-man *Schwarm* (Swarm) – these were the Luftwaffe's standard fighter formations. Once students had mastered them, they began practicing aerial combat, learning attack and defensive tactics for single aircraft and formations. The trainees were introduced to aerial gunnery, both air-to-ground and air-to-air, firing at ground targets and towed aerial targets. Student pilots often trained on pre-war fighter types like the Arado Ar 68 and Heinkel He 51, as well as the purpose-built Arado Ar 96 advanced trainer.

Toward the end of specialized training, students started flying the types of fighter aircraft they would employ in combat, although shortages of the most up-to-date models hampered training throughout the war, worsening as it went on. In the 1939–41 period, student fighter pilots would fly the earlier versions of the Bf 109 – B-, C-, D- and E-models. At the completion of their specialized fighter training, students would have accumulated a further 50 hours of flying time.

In 1940, the Luftwaffe relieved its training command of responsibility for operational training of new fighter pilots, instead setting up *Ergänzungstaffel* (Reserve

Training Squadron) or *Ergänzunggruppe* (Reserve Training Group) that were attached directly to a designated *Jagdgeschwader* (Fighter Wing). These reserve training units provided replacement pilots for the squadrons within the fighter wing. Here, newly minted fighter pilots received a final course of training in the latest tactics taught by experienced combat pilots.

At the reserve training units, young pilots reviewed and practiced formation flying and combat tactics, but more importantly benefited from the lessons their teachers had learned through hard fighting. Oberleutnant Walter Schuck, who joined the *Ergänzungstaffel* of JG 3 in October 1940 and went on to claim 206 victories flying with JGs 5 and 7, recalled a key lesson his instructors taught him:

> The highest priority of all, the instructors drummed into us time and time again, was to have the upper hand in the existing combat situation and keep a constant watch on the entire airspace in both vertical and horizontal planes. We were told to always remember that the victor in an air battle was usually the pilot who spotted the enemy first.

Following initial training and the award of a pilot's badge, trainees selected for fighters would start at a *Jagdfliegervorschulen*, before moving on to a *Jagdfliegerschule*. At these schools, student pilots would fly a variety of German and foreign aircraft to gain flying experience, before moving on to the operational aircraft they would fly in combat. Here, a trio of would-be *Jagdflieger* practice formation flying in Arado Ar 96Bs. The Luftwaffe's standard advanced trainer throughout the war, the Ar 96 was built in large numbers – a total of 2,891 examples were constructed by Arado, AGO, Avia and Letov. (Tony Holmes Collection)

As the war progressed and Luftwaffe losses mounted, it became difficult for the *Jagdfliegerschule* to obtain sufficient frontline operational aircraft. Many young fighter trainees, therefore, flew older versions of the Bf 109 like this B-model, allowing them to gain experience with the type and to practice flying in *Rotte* and *Schwarm* formations. (Tony Holmes Collection)

LOUIS E. CURDES

Nine-victory ace Louis Curdes claimed seven Bf 109s destroyed in combat, making him the highest scoring P-38 pilot against the aircraft in the Mediterranean during 1942–43. Born in Fort Wayne, Indiana, on November 2, 1919, he entered Purdue University upon graduating from high school, but after three years of studying joined the US Army Reserve on March 12, 1942 and was accepted for pilot training. Curdes completed his training at Luke Field, Arizona, and was commissioned as a second lieutenant on December 3, 1942, having accumulated 216 flying hours. He was assigned to the 329th FG (an operational training unit) based in Oakland, California, where he obtained an additional 28 hours of flying time in pursuit aircraft.

Transferred to the Mediterranean in early 1943, Curdes joined the 82nd FG's 95th FS. He made his first claims on April 29, 1943 during a sweep against Axis shipping. The 95th FS ran into a formation of Bf 109s, and in the ensuing combat Curdes was credited with three Bf 109s destroyed and a fourth damaged. He scored again on May 19, when he claimed two more Bf 109s over Sardinia. A month later, he claimed an Italian Macchi C.202 destroyed, again over Sardinia, and on July 30 damaged a Bf 109.

On August 27, Curdes was one of the 95th FS pilots escorting B-25s on a mission near Naples when enemy fighters attacked the formation. He claimed two Bf 109s shot down during the subsequent engagement, although one of his engines was damaged in the process. Heading home, Curdes' good engine was then hit by Flak and he was forced to crash-land on a beach south of Salerno, in Italy. Although captured by the Italians, he was a prisoner of war (PoW) for just a matter of days. After the Italian government signed an armistice on September 8, his jailers allowed Curdes and other American PoWs to escape. He spent eight months living behind German lines before finally making it back to Allied-held territory on May 27, 1944.

Promoted to the rank of captain and sent home, Curdes eventually joined the P-51D Mustang-equipped 3rd Air Commando Group, fighting in the Philippines, during early

2Lt Louis E. Curdes (Tony Holmes Collection)

1945. On February 7, he claimed a Mitsubishi Ki-46 "Dinah" destroyed, making him one of only three USAAF pilots to be credited with the destruction of German, Italian and Japanese aircraft. Curdes also had the unique experience of shooting down an American aircraft when he shot out the engine of a USAAF C-47 to prevent it from landing on a Japanese-held airstrip on Batan Island, in the Philippines. The 13 crew and passengers survived their ditching in the ocean nearby, and remarkably Curdes later married one of the nurses that had been on board.

Post-war, Curdes remained in the USAF and participated in the Berlin Airlift, retiring as a lieutenant colonel in 1963. He died in Fort Wayne on February 5, 1995

FRANZ SCHIESS

Franz Schiess was born on February 25, 1921 in St. Pölten, Austria. After joining the Wehrmacht, he saw service in the Polish campaign in September 1939. Schiess then transferred to the Luftwaffe, and underwent pilot training during 1940. On completion of his training, he was assigned to the *Geschwaderstab* of JG 53 on the Channel Front, flying his first combat mission on March 24, 1941. As a leutnant, Schiess participated in the invasion of the Soviet Union, codenamed Operation *Barbarossa*, claiming his first victories (an I-153 fighter and a DB-3 bomber) on the day the campaign commenced (June 22, 1941). Schiess had been credited with 14 victories on the Eastern Front by the time JG 53 was withdrawn to Germany in August 1941 and subsequently redeployed to Sicily.

Appointed *Geschwader* Adjutant in December 1941, Schiess flew operations over Malta, claiming 11 victories during 1942. In November, the *Stab* transferred to Tunisia, where he gained a further 13 victories. Flying the Bf 109G-2, Schiess claimed his first P-38 over Tunisia on December 3, 1942 for his 27th victory, claiming two more shot down 48 hours later. Known within JG 53 as an aggressive pilot, Schiess claimed six victories over Tunisia in January 1943 (including two P-38s). Promoted to oberleutnant the following month and given command of 8./JG 53 on Sicily, he led his *Staffel* on operations over Tunisia until the Axis capitulation in May.

Schiess claimed one more P-38 over Tunisia before the fighting shifted to the area around Sicily itself. Over the island, and nearby Pantelleria, Schiess claimed four P-38s shot down in the space of a week, with his victory of May 21 bringing his total claims to 50. On June 21 Schiess was awarded the Knight's Cross for 55 victories and was sent on leave for two months. He returned to 8./JG 53 in mid-August and participated in the fierce combats that took place over southern Italy. Promoted to hauptmann, Schiess was credited with downing seven P-38s between August 21–30, bringing his total claims against the Lightning to 17 – the most of any Luftwaffe pilot during the war.

On September 2, 1943, Schiess was shot down and killed in combat with Lightnings from the 82nd FG over the island of Ischia, in the Gulf of Salerno, while flying a Bf 109G-6. At the time of his death, he had completed 657 combat missions and claimed 68 victories.

Oberleutnant Franz Schiess (Tony Holmes Collection)

COMBAT

Bf 109 TACTICS

By the end of 1942, the *Jagdgruppen* had been at war for three years, refining the aerial combat tactics that Oberst Werner Mölders had developed during his time in Spain with the *Legion* Condor. The foundation of Luftwaffe fighter tactics was the principle of fighting in pairs, with a leader and wingman. Mölders had discovered that it was more effective to have one pilot concentrate on shooting down an enemy aircraft while a second pilot guarded his tail, allowing the leader to focus all his attention on the attack.

Mölders abandoned the more traditional formation of three aircraft flying in a close V. He found that two aircraft in a pair, with the wingman spread out from his leader, was better suited to high-speed aircraft like the Bf 109. Mölders developed the *Rotte* as the basic pair, with the *Rottenführer* (Pack Leader) as leader and responsible for initiating and carrying through attacks on enemy aircraft, and the *Rottenflieger* (Pack Flyer) or *Katschmark* protecting the leader's tail. The wingman flew some 650ft away and slightly behind the leader. In this formation, each pilot could cover the other's blind spot. Two *Rotte* made up a *Schwarm*, with the aircraft flying around 1,000ft apart, and the leading *Rotte* flying slightly ahead of the other. Larger formations of fighters were built up from combining multiple *Schwarm*.

Luftwaffe fighter pilots favored launching attacks on enemy aircraft from a higher altitude, often coming out of the sun, in a "dive-and-zoom" attack from the "four o'clock" to "eight o'clock" position until they were dead astern of the enemy aircraft.

A variation of this attack that some pilots used was what Generalleutnant Adolf Galland called the "up and under" attack, in which the pilot dived astern and below the enemy aircraft, coming in from under the pilot's blind spot to open fire. After a single firing pass, the pilot could use his diving speed to pull up to regain altitude for another attack.

An alternative to pulling back into a climb after the attack was the *Abschwung* (downturn), what American and British pilots called a "split-s". After firing at the enemy aircraft, the Luftwaffe pilot would roll his fighter inverted, execute a hard pull into a dive and then recover at a lower altitude, prior to climbing back up into a position from which to mount another attack. P-38 pilots in North Africa found that their German opponents rarely carried out repeated attacks, preferring "hit and run" passes lasting only a few seconds. If the German fighters lost the tactical advantage, they would break off their attack. Often, *Rotte* or *Schwarm* would attack in turn, so that if the first attack broke up an enemy formation, the second and subsequent attacks could hit stragglers or isolated elements.

Luftwaffe fighter tactics in World War II mirrored the principles of air combat set down by the great Hauptmann Oswald Boelcke, considered the father of air combat, in World War I. In his *Dicta Boelcke*, written in 1916, he said that fighter pilots should:

Always try to secure an advantageous position before attacking. Climb before and during the approach in order to surprise the enemy from above, and dive on him swiftly from the rear when the moment of attack is at hand.

Try to place yourself between the sun and the enemy. This puts the glare of the sun in the enemy's eyes and makes it difficult to see you and impossible for him to shoot with any accuracy.

Do not fire the machine guns until the enemy is within range and you have him squarely within your sights.

Attack when the enemy least expects it or when he is pre-occupied with other duties, such as observation, photography or bombing.

Never turn your back and try to run away from an enemy fighter. If you are surprised by an attack on your tail, turn and face the enemy with your guns.

These tactics worked particularly well against the P-38s, given, as will be seen, the bomber escort tactics the Lightning groups employed in the Mediterranean during 1942–43.

Luftwaffe pilots' opinions towards the P-38 varied. Oberstleutnant Heinz Bär, who commanded I./JG 77 in the fighting over Libya and Tunisia and claimed two P-38s shot down, did not consider the aircraft to be a difficult adversary, being easy to out-maneuver and a sure kill. In contrast, Oberstleutnant Johannes "Macki" Steinhoff who was *Kommodore* of JG 77 during the fighting over Sicily, developed a healthy respect for the P-38, particularly its formidable armament. He claimed four Lightning victories, but was in turn shot down by a P-38 later in 1944.

Bf 109G-2 COCKPIT

1. Revi C/12D reflector gunsight
2. Gunsight pad
3. Machine gun ammunition counters
4. Armament switch
5. Repeater compass
6. Artificial horizon/turn-and-bank indicator
7. Manifold pressure gauge
8. Tumbler switch
9. Canopy jettison lever
10. Main light switch
11. Instrument panel lights
12. Ignition switch
13. Start plug cleansing switch
14. Altimeter
15. Airspeed indicator
16. Tachometer
17. Propeller pitch position indicator
18. Fuel warning lamp
19. Combined coolant exit and oil intake temperature indicator
20. Starter switch
21. Fuel gauge
22. Undercarriage position indicator
23. Undercarriage control switch
24. Undercarriage switch
25. Undercarriage emergency release lever
26. Oil and fuel contents gauge
27. Throttle
28. Propeller pitch control
29. Dust filter handgrip
30. Bomb release button
31. Gun firing trigger
32. Control column
33. Drop tank contents indicator
34. Rudder pedals
35. Radiator cut-off handle
36. Ventilation control lever
37. Oil cooler flap control
38. Fuel cock lever
39. MG 151/20 cannon breech cover
40. Radiator shutter control lever
41. FuG 16ZY radio control panel
42. Drop tank pipe
43. Oxygen supply indicator
44. Oxygen pressure gauge
45. Radio control knob
46. Oxygen supply
47. Fuel injection primer pump
48. Tailplane incidence indicator
49. Undercarriage emergency lowering handwheel
50. Tailplane trim adjustment wheel
51. Seat
52. Radio tuner panel

Steinhoff considered the Lightning "a fast, low-profiled, fantastic fighter, and a real danger when it was above you. It was only vulnerable if you were behind it, a little below and closing fast, or turning into it, but on the attack [it was] a tremendous aircraft". Concerning the P-38's armament, Steinhoff said "certainly the effect was reminiscent of a watering can when one of these dangerous apparitions started firing tracer, and it was essential to prevent them from maneuvering into a position from which they could bring their guns to bear". The Lightning's ability to rapidly enter a climb, combined with its nose-mounted armament, negated the standard Luftwaffe tactic of pulling up after an attack. Instead, German pilots quickly learned to dive away from a P-38 so as to avoid the Lightning's concentrated fire.

Luftwaffe tactics worked less well against the B-17 and B-24 heavy bombers that the *Jagdgruppen* increasingly faced in the skies over Western Europe and the Mediterranean. Leutnant Johann Pichler, quoted earlier, claimed a B-17 shot down over Castel Benito, in Libya, in January 1943, but was frustrated with the armament of his Bf 109G-2:

> I had quickly discovered that the relatively light armament of my Bf 109G-2 – one 20mm cannon and two 7.9mm machine guns – was inadequate to seriously threaten such a heavyweight. Fitting a 2cm gondola weapon under each wing was not an entirely satisfactory solution, for while quite effective, the gondola weapons resulted in more weight and adversely affected the flying characteristics when we had to combat escort fighters. Even then it was possible to put burst after burst into a B-17 until all ammunition was exhausted, and still it would not go down.

A USAAF study of German fighter attacks on B-17s in the Northwest African theater from November 1942 to October 1943 found that the majority (35 to 60 percent) were from the rear, mostly from directly behind and level with the bomber formation. Frontal attacks were negligible. For some unknown reason, most German fighter attacks came either over the target or just after the bomber formation had turned for home, bombs gone, and rarely before.

The difficulty for bomber gunners was to judge timing and distance correctly when engaging a rapidly approaching fighter. Gunners opened fire, on average, when an enemy fighter was 663 yards away – for the attacking pilot, getting in closer increased the risk of being hit. German fighters could dive from a higher altitude, level off, open fire on a bomber and then pull up or dive away. Most pilots preferred to dive away, which meant they were only exposed to the ball turret gunner and possibly a waist gunner, avoiding the tail gunner. The other advantage was that if the fighter escorts attacked, as they usually did, the German pilot was already in a dive and building up speed to escape.

Veteran fighter pilot Oberstleutnant Johannes "Macki" Steinhoff saw combat throughout the war, completing 939 missions and being credited with 176 victories. Given command of JG 77 in March 1943, he led the unit in North Africa and then during the maelstrom of aerial combat over Sicily and Italy. Steinhoff, who fought Lightnings on a number of occasions, was credited with four P-38s destroyed on August 25, 1943 over Foggia, in Italy. (Tony Holmes Collection)

A Twelfth Air Force analysis of attacks on B-17 formations found that most enemy fighters approached from the tail position, coming in from the "five o'clock" to "seven o'clock" direction. During the period from June to September 1943, 35 to 60 percent of the attacks were against the tail. German fighter pilots sometimes used the tactic illustrated here to confuse the tail gunners. Four fighters would approach from behind the bomber formation to a distance of around 1,200–1,500 yards away. Two aircraft would break away 800 yards from the bombers, a third at 700 yards and the fourth at 600 yards. If a tail gunner followed one of the first fighters to break away, the others could then close in and fire on the bomber without fear of being hit by the twin 0.50-cal. machine guns in the tail turret.

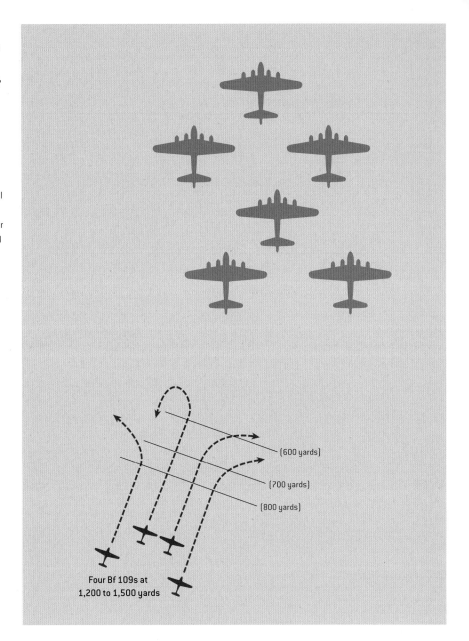

(600 yards)

(700 yards)

(800 yards)

Four Bf 109s at
1,200 to 1,500 yards

P-38 LIGHTNING TACTICS

The P-38 units arrived in North Africa (1st FG (27th, 71st and 94th FSs) and the 14th FG (48th and 49th FSs) in November, and the 82nd FG (95th, 96th and 97th FSs) in December 1942) with minimal experience of escorting bomber formations, no experience in aerial combat, and flying formations learned in training that were less effective in combat. In John Mullins' history of the 1st FG, *An Escort of P-38s*, Maj Joel Owens, who claimed five Bf 109s flying with the 27th FS (which he led from January 4, 1943), described the difficulties the squadrons faced:

The fighters ceded the initiative to the Luftwaffe as we committed to the role of close escort. We never seemed to get too close to suit the bombers. At times we put a flight in line abreast directly beneath the lead box of bombers. The idea was to compensate for the lack of forward firepower on the B-17s and to deter the enemy fighters from making sustained head-on attacks. We experimented with new formations and tactics almost daily in an effort to increase our effectiveness, and eventually settled on a loose finger-four formation for the individual flights, with the squadron right down on top of the bomber formation. Within the flight, if operating alone, the two elements would fly abreast and spaced widely enough to allow either element to turn inside and protect the other. The key word was protect. Even when our squadron fighter strength dwindled to the point that on December 15, 1942 two of us wound up escorting 18 B-17s on a mission to Tunis, we STAYED WITH THE BOMBERS!

In the beginning, we had little or no experience in bomber escort. Our formations and tactics clearly were not designed to attack and destroy enemy fighters. They were designed to prevent the bombers from being shot down by sustained attacks from enemy fighters. To that end, I believe we were successful, since the majority of bomber losses in the Tunisian campaign were due to anti-aircraft fire or mid-air collisions.

Capt (later Maj) Joel Owens, photographed with his 27th FS/1st FG P-38F in early 1943. By the end of the North African campaign, he had scored three victories while serving as CO of the 27th FS and two more with the 14th FG after he became the group's deputy CO. All five of his kills were Bf 109s. (Tony Holmes Collection)

The P-38 pilots in North Africa quickly learned that the keys to surviving a combat mission were to maintain a constant look-out for enemy fighters in all directions, rely on teamwork, keep formation discipline and skill in aerial gunnery. Finding the right type of formation to fly in combat depended on several variables, as a veteran P-38 pilot from one of the three P-38 groups with the Twelfth Air Force explained upon his return from North Africa:

The formation you fly depends on the type of mission you are on, the type of ship you are flying and the type of ship you expect to engage. In North Africa, when flying P-38Gs against Messerschmitt 109Gs and Focke-Wulf 190s, we had to use every possible advantage our ships had to combat them. We found out that we were about even in speed. In turning, they had such a high rate of roll they could beat us to the draw from a level start, but if we were already in a turn when they came in, we could out-turn them and, with our superior firepower, could meet them head-on with good results.

To gain the advantage of staying in a turn, we had to work out a constantly turning or weaving formation. It was possible to do this because we had plenty of gasoline and speed which could be used.

The formation we worked out which was very successful was a cross-weaving formation of two four-ship flights. We liked the two flights better than three because the third flight was left alone too much. This formation could be used for bomber escorts or fighter sweeps, and the sharpness of the turn depended on the probability of being attacked – in other words, if an attack was imminent the turns were sharper.

1. L-3 optical reflector gunsight
2. Hatch release handle
3. Hatch release buttons
4. Hatch locking arms
5. Cockpit light
6. Gun compartment heat control
7. 5-in. rockets fuse box
8. Standby magnetic compass
9. Suction gauge
10. Clock
11. Suction selector valve
12. Directional gyro
13. Gyro horizon
14. Dual manifold pressure gauge
15. Dual tachometer
16. Mixture controls
17. Coolant shutter controls
18. Throttle levers
19. Reserve fuel tank gauge
20. Altimeter
21. Airspeed indicator
22. Turn-and-bank indicator
23. Rate of climb indicator
24. Port engine oil temperature, oil pressure and fuel pressure gauge
25. Coolant temperature gauge
26. Carburetor air temperature gauge
27. Circuit breakers
28. Flap control lever
29. Radio on/off toggle switch and frequency selector push buttons
30. Recognition light switches
31. Elevator tab control
32. Bomb/tank release selector switches
33. Oxygen pressure gauge
34. Rudder pedals
35. Propeller feathering switch warning light
36. Oxygen flow indicator
37. Oxygen regulator
38. Parking brake handle
39. Free air temperature gauge
40. Control wheel
41. Control column
42. Aileron boost shut-off valve
43. Window crank handles
44. Landing gear extension/retraction control handle
45. Detrola radio beacon receiver tuning knob
46. Cockpit ventilator control
47. Port and starboard fuel tank selector valves
48. Outer wing tank low-level check button and auxiliary fuel pump switches
49. Seat adjustment lever
50. Seat
51. Machine gun button
52. Cockpit heat control
53. Propeller controls
54. Propeller selector switches
55. Microphone button
56. Fuel quantity gauge
57. Hydraulic pressure gauge
58. Oil cooler flaps position indicator
59. Landing gear and flaps position indicator
60. Fuel pressure warning lights
61. Machine gun and cannon blinker lights
62. Aileron trim tab control
63. Gun camera switch
64. Fuel pressure gauge
65. Armored glass and padded cushion

Typically, the B-17s flew at an altitude of 18,000–24,000ft as they approached their target, with the P-38 escort weaving several thousand feet above them. About ten minutes from the target, the P-38s would loosen up their formation and increase the number of turns they made around the bombers so as to ensure that they always provided a moving target to German fighters while still covering the bombers. As the B-17s began their bomb run, the P-38s would pull away to avoid the Flak, taking up a position up-sun as they flew around the Flak area, re-joining the bombers as their formation came out of the Flak area. The P-38s had to be alert for any stragglers the Flak might have damaged.

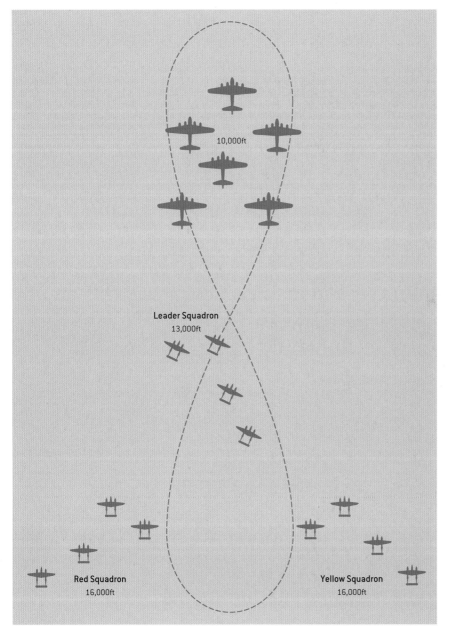

10,000ft

Leader Squadron
13,000ft

Red Squadron
16,000ft

Yellow Squadron
16,000ft

With little prior operational experience, the three P-38 groups in North Africa had to rapidly develop their own escort tactics. Typically, the leader of the escort formation would fly his squadron in a series of "figure-eights" about 3,000ft above the bomber formation. The second squadron, shown here as Red Squadron, would fly behind the bombers on the left side of the formation some 6,000ft above their charges, with the third squadron, shown here as Yellow Squadron, flying behind on the right and also 6,000ft above the bombers. The Leader Squadron would break up any concentrated attacks, with Red and Yellow Squadrons taking care of any fighters that broke through. The P-38s had to remain out of firing range of the bombers, which proved to be a handicap when trying to pursue enemy fighters attacking the bomber formation.

If the ratio of fighters to bombers was low, the fighters would make an offensive sweep of the target area before the bombers arrived, and would leave the target area after the last bomber formation had departed. The P-38 pilots were admonished that "no enemy fighters which are not in a position to attack the bombers should be allowed to draw [away] a section of the escort proper".

COMBAT

In the early clashes between the P-38 Lightnings and the Bf 109s in Tunisia, the Luftwaffe's more experienced pilots emerged victorious over and over again. It took time, and some painful losses, for the P-38 pilots to learn how to best employ the Lightning in combat with the Bf 109.

The 1st and 14th FGs arrived in North Africa in mid-November 1942, flying directly from England. Initially assigned to XII Fighter Command, the 1st FG was given the task of escorting B-17s of the 97th Bombardment Group (BG) from bases near Oran, with the 301st BG arriving towards the end of November. XII Fighter Command assigned the 14th FG's 48th and 49th FSs to a tactical role, supporting Allied forces advancing into Tunisia.

The 14th FG duly moved to the rough airfield – little more than a dirt strip – at Youks-les-Bains, on the Algerian–Tunisian border. From here, it began flying fighter sweeps, reconnaissance and strafing missions into Tunisia. The 1st FG's 94th FS joined the group for a few weeks in late November. The P-38 did well as an interceptor, and during the last week of November the 48th, 49th and 94th FSs claimed six Ju 88s and nine Italian SM.82 transports, the Germans losing approximately that number of Junkers bombers and the Regia Aeronautica seven of its transports.

The Lightnings did less well against Bf 109s. In the space of three days in early December, the 1st and 14th FGs lost 15 P-38s in combat with Bf 109s. The first confirmed encounter between the two types took place on November 28, when six P-38s from the 48th and 49th FSs ran into a formation of Bf 109s just after shooting down several Ju 52/3m transports. Each squadron lost one P-38 to the Messerschmitts. Later that day, Bf 109s badly damaged two more Lightnings, also from the 48th FS, while they were escorting Douglas A-20 Havoc light bombers of the 27th BG's 15th Bombardment Squadron (BS). Pilots from JGs 51 and 53 claimed seven P-38s shot down on the 28th. Among those to enjoy success was Hauptmann Friedrich-Karl Müller of I./JG 53, who was credited with the destruction of a P-38 for his 102nd victory.

1lt Virgil H. Smith, assigned to the 48th FS/14th FG, was one of the first P-38 pilots to see combat with Bf 109s over North Africa. He was later recognized as the first P-38 ace of the war, with six victories. Smith was credited with two victories over the Bf 109 (on November 30 and December 3) before he was killed on December 28, 1942 trying to land his damaged Lightning after making a claim for a third Bf 109. (3A-46962, RG 342FH, NARA)

Two days later, the 1st FG's 27th FS was escorting B-17s to Bizerte when Capt Joel Owen spotted what he identified as a "Me-109F" below him. Owen and his flight dived down to attack, and he fired a burst at the Messerschmitt as it half-rolled and dived away. As he stated in his combat report:

Almost immediately I sighted two Me-109Fs climbing. Lt Mendenhall and I dove to meet them. The enemy aircraft split, one turning left and the other right. I attacked the one to the right, employing a level attack from astern. I fired 350 rounds of 0.50-cal. and 5 rounds of 20mm into him. Obtaining hits, I saw cannon shells burst in his tail section. The enemy aircraft fell out of control, with a large volume of greyish white smoke pouring out. I believe I saw flames developing also.

During a mission on December 2, 1942, 1Lt Jack Ilfrey claimed two Bf 109s shot down, but lost his left engine to other Messerschmitts that attacked him. Ilfrey (see here standing on the left wing root next to the cockpit of his fighter) returned to base on his good right engine, demonstrating one of the best features of the P-38. Having two engines saved many a Lightning pilot from death or captivity. (208-03-31_image_585_01, Peter M. Bowers Collection, MoF)

5./JG 51 did indeed lose a Bf 109G-2/trop in the area, with a second example crash-landing after combat with these fighters. Later that afternoon, the 48th FS was on a reconnaissance mission when it ran into a formation of Bf 109s. 1Lt Virgil Smith claimed one shot down, but the squadron also lost a P-38.

On December 2 Capt Nowell Roberts led a flight of four 94th FS P-38s on a strafing mission to Sfax and Gabes. Coming in over Gabes airfield, they saw four Bf 109s taking off. Roberts targeted the first German fighter, while the rest of his flight took the remaining three. Soon after opening fire, six more Bf 109s jumped the P-38 flight. In the confused fighting that ensued, Roberts and 1Lt Jack Ilfrey claimed two Bf 109s each, with the other members of the flight claiming three more between them. Ilfrey had an engine shot out, but made it back to Youks-les-Bains. In this instance 5./JG 53 had a Bf 109 shot down, and two more that were so badly damaged as to be rendered unserviceable.

The following day, however, would see the 1st FG suffer badly at the hands of the Bf 109G-equipped *Jagdgeschwader*. The 27th FS sortied 14 P-38s, possibly with two aircraft from the 71st FS, to escort the 97th BG's B-17s attacking the docks at Bizerte. Over the target, ten Bf 109s bounced the Lightning formation, coming in from above and behind the USAAF fighters. One P-38 that was lagging behind was immediately shot down, while the rest of the formation became involved in a fierce dogfight. The Lightning pilots subsequently claimed three Bf 109s shot down, but lost four aircraft and had two pilots killed. The 71st FS may have lost an aircraft on this mission as well.

The 14th FG also lost several aircraft that day. On a fighter sweep to the Tunis area in the morning, the 48th FS ran into a formation of Bf 109s and Fw 190s. 1Lt Virgil

Feldwebel Anton "Toni" Hafner of II./JG 51 claimed two P-38s destroyed on December 18, 1942, and he subsequently met one of the pilots he shot down, 1Lt Norman Widen of the 94th FS/ 1st FG. This photograph, taken from the German wartime magazine *Signal*, shows Hafner holding Widen's flying helmet, standing next to the USAAF pilot who used burnt cork around his eyes to reduce the glare of the sun. As previously noted, Hafner was killed in action on October 17, 1944. In his will, he asked his brother to contact Widen, who survived as a PoW, and give him Hafner's German Cross in Gold and officer's dagger. His brother finally tracked Widen down in the early 1960s, by which point the former P-38 pilot was a major in the USAF. (Author's Collection)

Smith claimed a Bf 109 destroyed, but 2Lt Carl Williams was shot down and killed. In the afternoon, the 48th FS again ran into German fighters, losing two more P-38s, but the pilots survived and managed to return.

Overall, Lightning pilots claimed five Bf 109s shot down on December 3, but none were in fact lost. Their opponents, from II./JG 51 and *Stab* and I./JG 53, in turn claimed eight P-38s shot down – exactly the number lost that day. Among the successful Bf 109 pilots was Leutnant Franz Schiess, flying with *Stab.*/JG 53, who claimed a P-38 for his 27th victory. He would eventually become the leading Luftwaffe scorer against the Lightning.

The 27th FS sent out 19 P-38s on December 4 to escort the B-17s over Tunisia. Once again Bf 109s jumped the USAAF fighters, shooting down 1Lt David Everett and 2Lts Lawrence Pace and Hubert Black, who were all killed – a fourth P-38 was badly damaged and force-landed near Algiers. The next day, the 48th and 49th FSs were escorting A-20s from the 15th BS when ten to 15 Bf 109s and Fw 190s attacked. Six P-38s from the 49th FS turned into the attack, losing three pilots shot down and killed and two more forced to crash land after combat with the Bf 109s. Leutnant Franz Schiess added two claims to his growing score, the Bf 109 pilots of JGs 51 and 53 claiming eight P-38s shot down.

Thirteen days later, on December 18, the 1st FG suffered another heavy loss when escorting B-17s. On a mission to Bizerte, JGs 51 and 53 intercepted the American formation, damaging two B-17s that subsequently crash-landed on their way back to Allied territory and shooting down four P-38s from the 94th FS and one from the 27th FS. On December 30, the 48th FS lost three P-38s and their pilots in combat with the Bf 109s, one of which was flown by 1Lt Virgil Smith. Forty-eight hours earlier, he had become the first P-38 pilot in-theater to claim five enemy aircraft shot down.

During January 1943, the Lightning units continued to lose aircraft to the Bf 109 *Jagdgeschwader*. On the 23rd 16 aircraft of the 48th FS went on a strafing mission to Gabes, claiming 25 to 30 Axis vehicles destroyed prior to being bounced by Bf 109s from II./JG 51. A running fight ensued, during which the German pilots shot down four P-38s. Leutnant Herbert Puschmann of 6./JG 51 claimed one of the Lightnings for his 38th victory of the war.

The 82nd FG had arrived in North Africa at the end of December 1942 and began flying missions in early January. Towards the end of the month, on January 30, the group's 96th FS sent off 16 P-38s to escort 18 B-25s of the 310th BG to bomb El Aouinet, in Tunisia. Once again, Bf 109s from II./JG 51 bounced the formation, attacking continuously as the Lightnings covered the bombers as they withdrew back to Algeria. The 96th FS lost four P-38s to the German fighters, with a fifth crash-landing back at base when its landing gear failed to come down.

The squadron's pilots in turn claimed eight enemy fighters shot down, with 2Lt William Sloan being credited with his second Bf 109. II./JG 51, however, lost only one Bf 109, its pilot suffering fatal injuries while attempting to crash-land his damaged fighter. Eastern Front ace Oberfeldwebel Otto Schultz-Wittner downed two P-38s that day, with his fifth and sixth claims for P-38s that month being his 49th and 50th victories overall.

On January 31, during yet another escort mission, the 82nd FG's 97th FS lost two P-38s and the 27th FS one Lightning to the Bf 109s.

In a little over two months, the three P-38 fighter groups had lost an estimated 58 aircraft to the Bf 109 *Jagdgruppen*, in addition to losses to other Axis fighters and Flak. At the end of January, the 48th and 49th FSs, which between them had lost 31 aircraft to all causes and had had 27 pilots listed as killed, missing or captured, were withdrawn from combat and the 14th FG sent back to French Morocco to re-equip and reform. The three groups had claimed 53 Bf 109s shot down, with the 1st FG claiming 28, the 14th FG 14 and the 82nd FG 11.

Luftwaffe loss records present a very different picture, however. According to Jochen Prien's history of German fighter units (see Selected Sources), during this two-month period II./JG 51 lost one aircraft to the P-38s, JG 53 lost two and the recently committed JG 77 definitely lost one and possibly two to Lightnings. It is likely that the American pilots claimed far more Bf 109s than they actually shot down due to their inexperience in aerial combat. The *Jagdgruppen* Bf 109 pilots also claimed more P-38s than they actually shot down, being credited with the destruction of 92 Lightnings when they likely shot down 58. 1Lt Harry Crim, who flew with the 14th FG's 37th FS from early 1943 (and eventually became an ace flying P-51Ds in the Pacific in 1945), later recalled the problems P-38 pilots had confirming a claim:

In North Africa, the whole 37th FS started with just four gun cameras. The ground temperature was so high that the film melted, so from these four cameras I saw only about ten feet of developed footage. To claim a victory, you had to knock off a major piece of a plane (like a wing or the whole tail), set it on fire, or see it crash. You also had to have a confirming witness. With no gun camera film, the only witness was a member of your flight.

Our major enemy was the 109, which couldn't be set on fire above 16,000ft. It was a very strong airplane, and didn't shed parts very easily.

One victory sign was a bail out. The German pilots at altitude didn't have any incentive to take to their parachutes above 10,000ft, so you didn't expect it. The other criteria for a victory was to see the plane crash. Consider the problem from, say, 25,000ft. A 109 in a vertical dive at 400mph would require about

1Lt William "Dixie" Sloan of the 96th FS/82nd FG poses with his P-38G-5 42-12835 *Snooks IV½* near the end of his combat tour in August 1943, having accounted for eight German and four Italian aircraft between January 7 and July 22, 1943. Included in this tally were six Bf 109s destroyed and three damaged. Sloan remained the top USAAF ace in the Mediterranean theater until 1944. [Tony Holmes Collection]

On December 18, 1942, the 97th
and 301st BGs sent 36 B-17s, with
an escort of 16 P-38s from the
1st FG, to bomb the port at Bizerte.
Bf 109s from II./JG 51 and I./JG 53
intercepted the USAAF formation,
damaging two Flying Fortresses so
badly that they crash-landed in
Allied territory. Four Lightnings
were also shot down. Feldwebel
Anton Hafner, one of II./JG 51's
Experten, claimed two of the P-38s
destroyed. One of his victims was
1Lt Norman Widen, serving with the
94th FS, who was flying at 18,000ft
near the bombers when Hafner
bounced him from behind in his
Bf 109G-2/trop. Widen tried to
evade his pursuer, but when Hafner
set the Lightning on fire the
American had little choice but to
bail out. Landing close to Hafner's
airfield at Sidi Ahmed, Widen was
quickly captured and taken to meet
his victor.

a minute before it hit the ground. And in the skies over North Africa, Sicily or Italy, one minute taken out of a fight to watch a plane hit the ground would plant you right alongside him. Those boys weren't there to play.

Having withdrawn the 14th FG from its tactical role, the Twelfth Air Force decided that it made more sense to use the P-38s as escorts to bombers undertaking the growing interdiction campaign against Axis air power and lines of communications. During February–March 1943, the 1st and 82nd FGs devoted their efforts to escorting the B-17s, B-25s and B-26s on missions to targets in Tunisia and, for the first time, on Sardinia.

The P-38 pilots were learning and, with experience, becoming more effective. Having lost 27 P-38s to the Bf 109s during January, the 1st and 82nd FGs lost ten aircraft during February and 13 in March. While the Lightning pilots were still overclaiming (25 Bf 109s shot down in February and 39 in March), Bf 109 *Jagdgruppen* losses were indeed higher than they had been in previous months. During February and March the Bf 109 *Jagdgruppen* lost around 13 fighters to the P-38s. More importantly, the Lightnings were proving the value of close escort. While the B-25 and B-26 groups had approximately 16 aircraft downed by Axis fighters, the Germans and Italians only managed to shoot down two B-17s, although more were damaged in fighter attacks.

The 82nd FG flew a difficult mission of February 8, sending 18 P-38s to escort B-25s from the 310th BG and B-26s from the 17th BG tasked with bombing airfields around Gabes (four of the Lightnings had to turn back). A large force of Axis fighters intercepted the USAAF formation and a furious dogfight erupted. Turning constantly, the P-38s managed to shoot down two Bf 109s from 6./JG 51 and one from III./JG 77 (Lightning pilots claimed nine Bf 109s shot down) for the loss of one P-38.

Their opponents also over-estimated their success, claiming nine P-38s shot down. On this mission the Lightnings were too few in number to provide full protection to the bombers, resulting in the 310th BG losing four B-25s to Axis fighters, with a fifth crash-landing back at base.

During March the P-38 groups had particular success against JG 53, with the German unit probably losing six Bf 109s to the Lightnings. On the 8th, the 1st FG's 27th and 71st FSs escorted the 97th BG's B-17s when they targeted shipping off Bizerte, with some 20 Bf 109s and Fw 190s protecting the Axis convoy. In a series of fierce combats, the P-38 pilots claimed eight German fighters destroyed, five probables and three damaged. In reality, 5./JG 53 had two Bf 109s shot down. Given the multiplicity of claims, it is next to impossible to determine which P-38 pilot actually shot down the two Bf 109s that were lost.

Two days later, the 94th FS shot down another Bf 109 from I./JG 53 while escorting 72 B-17s from the 97th and 301st BGs sent to bomb El Aouina and La Marsa airfields. A solitary P-38 was lost.

Later in March, the 82nd FG again engaged fighters from JG 53, shooting down a single Bf 109 during the course of two missions, although many more were claimed. The first clash occurred on the 20th, when the 96th FS escorted B-25s from the 321st BG as the

Oberleutnant Wolfgang Tonne, *Staffelkapitän* of 3./JG 53, claimed two P-38s destroyed in March 1943 during the ill-fated defense of Tunisia. On April 20, having just claimed three Spitfires shot down in a single mission (taking his overall tally to 120 victories), Tonne perished in a landing accident. (Tony Holmes Collection)

medium bombers conducted a sea sweep in search of an Axis convoy. A force of enemy fighters attacked the P-38s, who subsequently claimed eight Bf 109s shot down. 6./JG 53 lost one fighter, and claimed three P-38s shot down. Two of these were credited to Oberfeldwebel Rudolf Ehrenberger for his 29th and 30th victories. Ehrenberger had made his first claim for an enemy aircraft destroyed during the Battle of Britain. In this case, however, only one P-38 had been damaged in combat, although it was written off in a crash landing.

The 82nd FG ran into JG 53 again on March 22 when the 95th FS escorted B-26s from the 17th BS on another shipping sweep. The P-38s fought a group of Axis fighters escorting a convoy, claiming nine Bf 109s shot down. 2Lt Richard Hattendorf claimed one shot down, while his brother, 2Lt Wilbur Hattendorf, who also flew with the 95th FS, claimed a second Bf 109 as a probable. The 95th lost three P-38s, one of which was a straggler shot down by Oberleutnant Wolfgang Tonne for his 113th victory claim. JG 53 pilots were credited with seven P-38s shot down for the loss of one Bf 109 from 3./JG 53. The following day, the 1st FG escorted B-17s to Bizerte, claiming three Bf 109s for the loss of a P-38. Once again, JG 53 lost a Bf 109 from *Stab* II./JG 53.

As Allied ground forces pressed the Axis in Tunisia from east and west and air attacks on Axis shipping became increasingly effective, the Luftwaffe and the Regia Aeronautica resorted to bringing supplies and troops in to Tunisia by air. In early April, the Allies launched Operation *Flax* – a concerted effort to intercept Axis transport aircraft flying from Sicily and southern Italy to Tunisia. While the Twelfth Air Force's B-17s continued to bomb harbor facilities, shipping and airfields in Tunisia and on Sicily, the medium bombers carried out sweeps against Axis shipping and transport aircraft, with P-38 escorts. High losses of German and Italian transport aircraft meant that they had to be provided with fighter escorts, thus stretching the demands being made on the *Jagdgruppen* even further.

OPPOSITE

Pilots of 4./JG 53 stage a mock *Alarmstart* (emergency scramble) for visiting journalists at La Marsa airfield near Tunis. "White 5" was the aircraft of Oberfeldwebel Stefan Litjens, who made his first claim with JG 53 in April 1940. Severely wounded in combat with Russian fighters in September 1941, he returned to frontline flying 14 months later despite having lost his right eye. Litjens, who claimed three P-38s destroyed flying with 4./JG 53, had taken his overall tally to 32 when he was badly wounded for a second time when attacking a B-17 in March 1944. (B.A. Bild 1011-421-2056-34)

The Bf 109G-2/4 was equipped with the Revi C 12/D reflector gunsight, which could be used for fixed gunnery and bombing. The G-models used the KG 13A firing grip on the control column to operate the nose machine guns and the engine-mounted cannon, as well as the underwing gondola cannon if mounted. Anxious to avoid the concentrated fire from the P-38's nose-mounted cannon and machine guns, Bf 109 pilots fighting over Tunisia and Sicily quickly learned never to approach a Lightning head-on or to pull up in front of the aircraft after an attack. The P-38 was, however, vulnerable if engaged from the rear and slightly below – a blind spot for Lightning pilots.

During April, the 1st and 82nd FGs had several encounters with both JG 53 and II./JG 27, which had returned to combat in-theater. While the latter *Gruppe* probably lost three fighters to the P-38s and JG 53 at least one, the Bf 109 pilots fought back hard, inflicting 11 losses on the 82nd FG in two encounters.

On April 5 – the first day of Operation *Flax* – the 1st FG escorted B-25s on a sea sweep, running into a formation of Ju 52/3m transports with an escort of Bf 109s, Bf 110s and several other aircraft. Shortly thereafter, the 82nd FG, also on a sweep

over the same area, joined in the attacks on the transports and the escorting fighters. In the confused fighting that followed, the P-38 squadrons claimed 20 Ju 52/3ms and six Bf 109s, among other aircraft, shot down. In return, the 1st FG's 27th FS lost two P-38s to the German fighters, while the 96th and 97th FSs of the 82nd FG suffered the loss of four aircraft. 4./JG 53, which was escorting the transports, claimed five P-38s shot down for no loss.

Later that day the 95th FS escorted B-25s to bomb a landing ground in western Sicily, where Bf 109s from 4./JG 27 intercepted them. The German unit reported two Bf 109s lost to the P-38s, although only 2Lt Wilbur Hattendorf claimed a fighter shot down.

In the weeks that followed, the P-38s had several encounters with Axis transports and their escorts, the 1st FG claiming five Bf 109s shot down and the 82nd FG no fewer than 21, for the loss of 16 P-38s.

At the end of the month, the 82nd was hit hard again during two missions flown on April 29. The first of these saw the 97th FS escort B-25s on a sea sweep that was intercepted by Bf 109s from II./JG 27. Two P-38s were shot down, although one of the victors, Leutnant Bernhard Schneider (an ace with 21 victories to his name), in turn fell to either 2Lt Robert Congdon or 1Lt Joe Henley, both of whom submitted claims for a Bf 109. Congdon, who had joined the 97th FS just 24 hours earlier and was on his first combat mission flying as wingman to 1Lt Merle "Swede" Larson, described his experiences in Steve Blake's history of the 82nd FG, *Adorimini – "Up and at 'Em!"*:

Groundcrew push a Bf 109G-4 belonging to II./JG 27 back into its revetment. After rest and re-equipment, II./JG 27 returned to combat from airfields in southern Sicily, escorting transport flights to Tunisia. (B.A. Bild 1011-421-2070-29)

P-38 pilots flying against Bf 109s in Tunisia found that they could compensate for the Lightning's relatively poor rate of roll if they were already in a turn. Some squadrons worked out what they called a "crossweaving" formation, similar to the US Navy's Beam Defense Formation – better known as the "Thach Weave" after its originator, Lt Cdr John Thach. Two flights of P-38s would fly a weaving course, crossing over and under each other as they continued to weave. If enemy aircraft attacked "A" Flight, then "B" Flight would remain in its turn and fire on the Axis fighter targeting "A" Flight, continuing the weave.

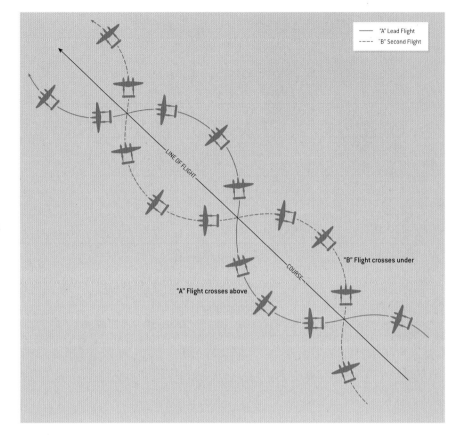

"A" Lead Flight
"B" Second Flight

LINE OF FLIGHT

COURSE

"B" Flight crosses under

"A" Flight crosses above

We took off as scheduled. I jockeyed into position and held a very tight formation (I was scared). We picked up a group of B-25s and started for targets of opportunity in the Sicilian Straits. My radio was buzzing loudly so I turned it off, as I thought I could be transmitting – breaking radio silence was "verboten".

It seemed like [only] a few seconds [later] when "Swede" broke sharply left and, at the same time, dropped his belly tanks. I hit the switch to drop mine and managed to get the radio on. Our element leader and wingman were both hit and went down.

The squadron immediately started weaving in two-ship elements. We were on the deck one moment and, in the next moment, at several thousand feet. Calls were coming in [such] as "Twelve o'clock high". I had never experienced the excitement of combat. All I knew was that I had to stay with "Swede".

All of a sudden another call came in – a bandit was coming in on our element. We turned into him and "Swede" gave him a burst and pulled off. As the 109 banked away, I had him in my gunsight and pressed both buttons, firing my 0.50s and my 20mm cannon. I saw tracers going into him and then pulled away, as I didn't want to lose "Swede". My machine guns were still firing, and I thought I had runaway machine guns and cannon. I realized that my fingers were frozen on the firing buttons! I reached over with my left hand and pried them loose.

Fortunately, I caught up with "Swede". Since we saw no targets of opportunity, we regrouped and headed back. At the debriefing, one pilot mentioned that he saw two 38s firing into a 109. The first pulled away and the second, which he identified as my ship,

"CS", continued firing and the 109 started trailing smoke and dove into the Mediterranean. I was questioned rather closely, and I told the debriefing officers I remembered firing at several 109s, but my main thought was to stay on "Swede's" wing. Since it was verified, I was credited with a victory on my first mission.

Later that day, the 95th FS went on an anti-shipping mission, with each aircraft carrying one 500lb bomb and a drop tank. The P-38s ran into a large formation of Bf 109s apparently from 5. and 6./JG 27, as well as elements from JG 53. A confused combat then followed, with the 95th FS pilots claiming six Bf 109s shot down – 2Lt Louis Curdes was credited with three destroyed and three probables. The 95th lost three P-38s shot down in the action, with two more crash-landing east of Algiers, including the fighter flown by Curdes. JG 27 suffered no losses in this combat, but JG 53 reported two Bf 109s missing.

Two weeks later, all Axis forces in Tunisia surrendered. Attention quickly shifted to the next stage of the Allied advance, the invasion of Sicily. The first priority of the air offensive in support of Operation *Husky* was to neutralize Axis air forces within range of Sicily. This entailed regular attacks on Axis airfields in Sardinia, Sicily and southern Italy. In addition the Twelfth Air Force's heavy and medium bomber groups continued to target Axis lines of communication, hitting key ports and shipping facilities. The Twelfth Air Force's units operating under NASAF control were to concentrate their attacks on Sardinia and western Sicily, while the Ninth Air Force covered eastern Sicily and southern Italy. Attacks on Axis airfields in Sardinia and Sicily began even before the fall of Tunisia.

Bf 109Gs from 5./JG 53 sit in their rudimentary, camouflaged revetments at Comiso, on Sicily, in early May 1943 following the unit's recent withdrawal from La Marsa. (Tony Holmes Collection)

After spending three months receiving new aircraft and replacement pilots, the 14th FG returned to combat in May 1943. Here, pilots of the 49th FS synchronize their watches before heading out on a mission. (3A-29044, RG 342FH, NARA)

In early June, the Twelfth Air Force decided to organize its bomber units into wings based on their type of aircraft, and to assign specific fighter groups to each wing to act as escorts. The 5th Bomb Wing (BW) contained all B-17 units, with the 2nd and 99th BGs joining the 97th and 301st BGs. The 1st FG and the renewed 14th FG, which returned to combat in early May with three full squadrons (37th, 48th and 49th FSs), were assigned to the 5th BW. The 82nd FG went to the 47th BW, which controlled the 310th and 321st BGs with B-25s. However, in practice, the three P-38 groups were interchangeable, and sometimes escorted other formations outside their assigned wing. With three full groups of P-38s, the Twelfth Air Force now had more than 500 P-38s available, including aircraft held in reserve. By this point in the war the Lightning groups were receiving a steady flow of replacement aircraft and better trained pilots.

Their Luftwaffe adversaries were in a worse position following the Axis debacle in Tunisia. Between November 1942 and May 1943, the Luftwaffe had lost 2,422 aircraft in the Mediterranean, including 888 fighters, shot down, destroyed on the ground or abandoned on Tunisian airfields. In the hasty retreat from North Africa the *Jagdgruppen* left behind tons of equipment, spare parts and groundcrew. By mid-May 1943, the Luftwaffe had just 180 single-engined fighters available in the central Mediterranean. By dint of effort, on the eve of the invasion of Sicily the number of single-engined fighters (day fighters, fighter-bombers and ground attack fighters) had increased to 480 aircraft, despite losses of 131 fighters during June.

As reinforcements for the beleaguered *Jagdgruppen* that had retreated from Tunisia, the Luftwaffe brought in a new Bf 109 *Gruppe*, IV./JG 3, retained II./JG 27 and II./JG 51 and replenished aircraft and pilots in JGs 53 and 77 by bringing their three *Gruppen* more or less up to full strength. The more potent Bf 109G-6 version replaced older G-2 and G-4 aircraft. The nine Bf 109 *Gruppen* based in Sardinia, Sicily and southern Italy were, just before the Sicilian invasion, equipped with around 300 Bf 109s, of which 165 were serviceable. In total, the Luftwaffe and the Regia Aeronautica could field between 1,500–1,600 aircraft to counter more than 3,000 Allied combat aircraft.

The *Jagdgruppen* still had many *Experten* flying against the Allies, among them Leutnant Franz Schiess, who in February 1943 had been promoted to oberleutnant and placed in command of 8./JG 53. By April Schiess had claimed six P-38s shot down, and he would add another four during May. He made his first claim of the month for a P-38 on May 18, when II./JG 27 and III./JG 53 engaged in an intensive fight with the 14th FG, which had returned to combat two weeks earlier.

On this date the 14th's 37th and 48th FSs were escorting 97th BG B-17s targeting Trapani, on Sicily, when Bf 109s intercepted them. Nine P-38s and two B-17s were subsequently claimed to have been shot down, although no bombers were in fact lost. Schiess claimed one P-38, while Major Gustav Rödel, *Kommodore* of JG 27, claimed a P-38 and a B-17 shot down to take his tally to 75. 7./JG 53 lost one fighter to the Lightnings. The 14th FG claimed five Bf 109s shot down, with future ace 1Lt Richard Campbell being credited with two, but lost two P-38s from the 37th FS, one from the 48th FS and one from the headquarters flight of the group flown by Maj Clarence Tinker, the 14th FG's Executive Officer. Two more P-38s returned to base with one engine shot out.

On May 19 the 14th FG again escorted 97th BG B-17s, the bombers attacking Milo airfield near Trapani. In a repeat of the previous day, II./JG 27 and III./JG 53 intercepted the American formation. The 14th FG's 49th FS claimed three Bf 109s as probably shot down, and 7./JG 53 reported two pilots missing following the combat. The 49th also lost two pilots on the mission, Oberleutnant Schiess being one of several Bf 109 pilots to make a claim for a P-38, taking his victory tally to 49.

That same afternoon the 82nd FG's 95th FS escorted B-25s from the 321st BG in a raid on Villacidro airfield on Sardinia. As the formation was withdrawing, eight Bf 109s apparently from 9./JG 53 attacked. In the combat that followed, the P-38 pilots claimed five fighters shot down, with three probables and two damaged. Although 2Lt Louis Curdes was credited with two Bf 109s for his fourth and fifth victories, it appears that 9./JG 53 lost only one fighter, and this may have been to P-40s of the 325th FG, who were escorting B-25s bombing another airfield nearby.

Schiess was in action against the P-38s again on May 21 when the 14th FG escorted 97th and 99th BG B-17s to bomb Castelvetrano airfield on Sicily. II./JG 27 and III./JG 53 intercepted the formation, claiming three B-17s and four P-38s shot down. Once again there were no bombers lost. Schiess claimed one of the P-38s for his 50th. Although pilots from the 14th FG thought the German fighters were not aggressive,

1Lt Richard Campbell, who joined the 37th FS in January 1943 as an attrition replacement for the badly mauled 14th FG, was credited with two Bf 109s shot down and one damaged on May 18 for his first claims. Following a Bf 109 probable ten days later, a C.202 destroyed on June 15 and a Bf 109 downed on July 9, Campbell claimed two more Bf 109s shot down and a third damaged on August 28 for the final claims of his tour. (3A-46979, RG 342FH, NARA)

two P-38s were lost and only two Bf 109s damaged in return. Schiess wrote about the action in a letter to his family:

> The day before yesterday I got my 50th. It was another combat with about 60 enemy fighters, but this time we were roughly equal in number. I led my *Staffel* into a group of 20 aircraft and scattered them. The American fighters tried to run for safety. I hit one in the left engine. A second American tried to protect this cripple, and I positioned myself about 30m behind him. A brief burst sufficed and he went down in flames and crashed into the sea near Pantelleria. The one I crippled was then finished off by an unteroffizier of my *Staffel*. These days, the Americans always get such a pasting when they come to Sicily that they will soon lose their desire. Of course, there was a big celebration to mark my 50th, and the entire *Staffel*, from kapit*ä*n to airman, got completely loaded.

Unfortunately for Schiess and his comrades, the USAAF did not lose its desire to attack Sicily. On May 25, Schiess led his *Staffel* in the interception of a large formation of B-17s bombing Messina, with the Flying Fortresses being escorted by the 1st FG. He claimed one of the three P-38s credited to III./JG 53 that day, with no losses in return. Pilots from the 27th and 71st FSs, however, claimed nine Bf 109s shot down for the loss of three P-38s, with a fourth badly damaged. This was Schiess' tenth Lightning victory, and his total had been matched on May 31 by Oberfeldwebel Otto Schultz-Wittner of 4./JG 51 – his P-38 kill on this date had taken his overall victory tally to 55.

As Schiess had boasted in his letter home, the Bf 109 *Gruppen* had maintained their dominance over the P-38s in May 1943. The 1st FG had lost perhaps five aircraft to the Bf 109s while the 14th FG had suffered 14 losses, with the Luftwaffe having nine Bf 109s destroyed in return. Nevertheless, the Bf 109 *Gruppen* failed in what should have been their primary task – destroying USAAF bombers. During May the Ninth and Twelfth Air Force heavy bomber units had a loss rate, based on aircraft shot down by enemy fighters as a percentage of effective sorties, of less than one percent; the figure for medium and light bombers was the same. Although the P-38 groups appear to have lost more aircraft than the number of Bf 109s they shot down, they repeatedly kept Axis fighters away from the bombers they were escorting. This was to cause a crisis for the *Jagdgruppen* during June.

For the first 12 days of the month, the Allies concentrated on bombing Pantelleria, southwest of Sicily. After the Italian garrison on the island surrendered on June 13, the Twelfth Air Force's heavy and medium

Four pilots from the 27th FS/ 1st FG who claimed German fighters shot down on May 25, 1943 over Sicily. They are, from left to right, 2Lts John Mackay (two Bf 109 – these victories made him and ace), Samuel Sweet (two Bf 109s), Warren Holden (two Fw 190s) and Frank McIntosh (two Bf 109s). They are standing in front of Mackay's P-38G. (3A-23511, RG 342FH, NARA)

bombers returned to targeting Axis airfields on Sardinia and Sicily, shifting to bombing industrial targets and port facilities towards the end of the month. In the weeks after the fall of Pantelleria, Axis aircraft downed four B-26s and one B-17. Several more were damaged and had to crash land back at their airfields in Algeria.

In the fighting over Pantelleria, the 1st FG had claimed five Bf 109s shot down on June 9, with 1Lt Daniel Kennedy claiming three destroyed and one damaged, although apparently the only Bf 109 lost that day fell in combat with B-24s of the Ninth Air Force.

This P-38 from the 27th FS/1st FG was damaged in combat with Bf 109s from JG 77 over Sicily on June 20, 1943. Its pilot, 1Lt Herbert McQuown, was wounded when a bullet entered the cockpit, glanced off the instrument panel and hit him in the leg. (3A-28501, RG 342FH, NARA)

The next clash took place on June 18 when the 1st and 82nd FGs escorted B-26s and, later, B-25s to Sardinia, where a mixed force of German and Italian fighters intercepted the bombers. In the early mission, Axis fighters did shoot down two B-26s, but the B-25s suffered no losses. The 1st FG, which had gone in earlier, claimed two Bf 109s destroyed, a probable and a damaged for the loss of one P-38. The 82nd FG's 96th FS claimed a whopping 17 Italian and German fighters (including two Bf 109s) destroyed, and also lost one P-38. Again, no Bf 109s were lost in combat, although several Italian fighters were shot down or damaged.

Two days later, the 1st and 14th FGs escorted B-26s sent to Castelvetrano airfield on Sicily, running into I. and II./JG 77 and Italian fighters during the course of the mission. The 1st FG claimed 14 Bf 109s shot down, with 2Lt Harold Lentz being credited with three victories, while losing three P-38s. The 14th FG claimed three Bf 109s for no loss. JG 77 lost two Bf 109s in the encounter, one from each *Gruppe*, while claiming four P-38s shot down.

All three Lightning groups escorted the B-25s and B-26s to Sardinia again on 24 June, battling the Bf 109s of JG 77. The 1st FG claimed eight Bf 109s shot down while the 14th FG was credited with seven, for the loss of three 1st FG P-38s and two from the 14th FG. Once again, the bombers suffered no losses to enemy fighters, III./JG 77 losing one Bf 109. The next day, 123 B-17s attacked Messina in the largest concentration of American four-engined bombers to date. Axis fighters claimed 11 B-17s shot down, but none were lost – one crash-landed back at base. A furious *Reichsmarschall* Hermann Göring, incensed at the *Jagdgruppen*'s failure to shoot down more American bombers, ordered that one pilot from each *Jagdgruppe* that took part in the interception be tried for cowardice – a step that did nothing to improve morale among hard-pressed Luftwaffe fighter pilots.

Following the invasion of Sicily on July 10, 1943, the P-38s contributed to the air umbrella the MAAF placed over the island, carrying out 829 patrols and ground support sorties between July 10–12 and losing 11 aircraft. The Lightnings returned to escorting the heavy and medium bombers to targets in Sicily and Italy a week or so later. There were fewer encounters with the Bf 109 *Gruppen* during the month, the 14th FG claiming 14 Bf 109s shot down and the 82nd FG just six. Promoted in May, now-1Lt William Sloan claimed his final Axis aircraft during the month, including Bf 109s on July 5 and 22, making him the leading Twelfth Air Force pilot against the German fighter with six claims (from a total of 12 victories). He would hold this unacknowledged title for a little over a month.

In the duels between the P-38 and the Bf 109, August 1943 proved to be a month of intense combat and heavy losses for the Lightning groups. During the month, the Bf 109s probably shot down 42 P-38s – the greatest number of losses the Lightning groups experienced during their time with the Twelfth Air Force. The 1st FG was hit particularly hard, suffering its worst day in combat when the group lost 13 P-38s during a single mission.

The leading aces of the 82nd FG in the summer of 1943. They are, from left to right, 1Lt Ward Kuentzel (three Bf 109 victories), Flt Off Frank Hurlbut (two Bf 109s victories), 1Lt Ray Crawford (three Bf 109s victories), 2Lt Lawrence Liebers, 1Lt William Sloan (six Bf 109 victories) and 2Lt Louis Curdes (seven Bf 109 victories). (Tony Holmes Collection)

In attempting to counter the Allied invasion of Sicily, the Bf 109 units took a hammering, losing many aircraft on the ground to Allied bombing and heavy losses in personnel to Allied fighters and anti-aircraft fire. The newly-arrived IV./JG 3 lost five pilots, JG 53 had nine pilots killed and JG 77 had no fewer than 19 pilots killed or captured. Even the *Experten* had difficulty surviving, while new replacement pilots often failed to return from their first contact with, by now, their more experienced opponents. Yet, despite their losses, the *Jagdgruppen* continued to fight hard. In the heavy combats during August, the P-38 pilots reported that the enemy aircraft were persistent and very aggressive in their attacks, leading some to wonder if the Luftwaffe had brought in fresh, elite units.

The first of these intense encounters took place on August 20 when the 1st FG escorted two groups of B-26s to bomb marshaling yards at Caserta, on Sicily, while the 82nd FG escorted B-25s to bomb Benevento, near Naples. The 1st FG's P-38s were covering the bombers at 13,000ft when Axis fighters started making attacks from above, concentrating on the tail-end flight formation and coming in to attack in pairs and in threes. The 27th and 94th FSs claimed eight Bf 109s shot down, but lost five P-38s in the process to II. and III./JG 53.

An hour later, the 82nd FG ran into enemy fighters, claiming three Fw 190s and a single Bf 109, but losing three P-38s. IV./JG 3 was also involved in these combats, claiming five Lightnings shot down for no loss. One of the successful claimants was Feldwebel Hans Feyerlein of 6./JG 53, who was credited with two P-38s shot down for his 14th and 15th victories of the war, and his seventh and eighth claims for Lightnings. Oberleutnant Franz Schiess also claimed a P-38 that day.

The 1st FG lost a further four Lightnings in combat with Axis fighters on 28 August, IV./JG 3 and JG 53 claiming eight shot down, with Schiess being credited with two. The previous day, the 82nd FG's 2Lt Louis Curdes had claimed two Bf 109s during an escort mission to Benevento before being shot down and taken prisoner. This brought his total Bf 109 victories to seven, thus making him the leading Twelfth Air Force P-38 pilot against the Messerschmitt fighter.

The mission for the 1st FG on August 30 was to escort B-26s to bomb the marshaling yards at Aversa, just north of Naples. All three of the group's squadrons participated in the mission. As the formation crossed the coast on the way to the target, the P-38 pilots saw a larger group of Axis fighters approaching in two waves. They dropped their tanks and turned towards the enemy fighters. The returning P-38 pilots stated that their opponents were very aggressive, concentrating their attacks on the fighters and keeping up the attacks until the P-38s were well out to sea after the bombing.

The harassed P-38 pilots claimed seven Bf 109s shot down, but 13 Lightnings were lost, with the 27th and 71st FSs suffering four losses and the 94th FS five. IV./JG 3, II. and III./JG 53 and I./JG 77 claimed 26 P-38s shot down for the loss of four Bf 109s, Oberleutnant Schiess being credited with two P-38s for his 16th and 17th (and final) claims against the Lightning. Remarkably, the two B-26s groups participating in the mission suffered no losses. For its tenacity in defending the bombers, the 1st FG was awarded the DUC.

Three days later, on September 2, the 82nd FG suffered its heaviest losses of the war in another intense combat with Bf 109s from IV./JG 3, II. and III./JG 53 and

Comiso airfield was rendered unusable by a B-24 raid on June 17, with II./JG 53 being particularly badly hit by the devastating attack. Amongst the aircraft found by the Allies at the airfield upon its capture was this Bf 109G-6, which had been damaged taking off from Comiso on May 26. (Tony Holmes Collection)

I./JG 77. That day, the 82nd was escorting 72 B-25s targeting the marshaling yards at Cancello, north of Naples. For some reason, Axis fighters did not intercept the formation until after the bombers had hit their target and turned for the coast. The 96th FS turned in to the attacking fighters and was soon engaged in an intense dogfight. The 95th FS turned back to help, and also became heavily involved as the combat dropped down to 4,000ft over the Bay of Naples. A short time later, the 97th FS left the bomber formation, now racing to safety, to help its fellow squadrons. The fighting went on until 75 miles from the Italian coast.

By the time the German fighters broke off their attacks, ten 82nd FG pilots were missing in action, with the 96th FS losing seven P-38s. The three squadrons claimed 23 enemy fighters shot down, including 15 Bf 109s, with 2Lt Fred Selle claiming three destroyed and two damaged. The Bf 109 *Gruppen* lost six aircraft in combat with the P-38s, three of them from JG 53. Amongst those killed was Franz Schiess, who had been awarded a Knight's Cross in June and recently promoted to hauptmann. Schiess was last seen pursuing the P-38s well out to sea.

The Axis fighters failed to shoot down a single bomber thanks to the determined defense mounted by the P-38 pilots. Like the 1st FG on August 30, the 82nd FG received a DUC for its pilots' exceptional determination in defending the bombers at a high cost to themselves. This mission proved to be the last significant combat between P-38s and Bf 109s until organizational changes brought the Lightning groups to a new battlefield.

STATISTICS AND ANALYSIS

The claims made for opposing fighters shot down were remarkably similar between the P-38 and Bf 109 units. Based on historian Frank Olynyk's extensive research into credits for the destruction of enemy aircraft in the Mediterranean Theater of Operations during World War II, between November 1942 and early September 1943, the three Twelfth Air Force P-38 fighter groups claimed about 345 Bf 109s destroyed in aerial combat. The 1st and 82nd FGs each claimed 128 Bf 109s shot down. The 14th FG, which was withdrawn from combat from the end of January through to early May 1943, claimed 89 Bf 109s. The leading P-38 squadron in terms of aerial victories was the 82nd FG's 96th FS with claims for 47 Bf 109s, with the 1st FG's 94th FS just behind with 46 claims. The two leading scorers against the Bf 109 were the 95th FS's 2Lt Louis Curdes with seven claims and 1Lt William Sloan from the 96th FS with six claims.

According to research by Jochen Prien and his colleagues for the study of the Luftwaffe fighter force in World War II (see Further Reading), the Luftwaffe's Bf 109 *Gruppen* claimed, in turn, about 360 P-38s shot down between November 1942 and September 1943. The leading *Geschwader* was JG 53, which had three *Gruppen* in action for the entire period. Its pilots claimed 170 P-38s shot down, with III./JG 53 being credited with 66 and II./JG 53 63. 6. and 9./JG 53 were both tied with claims for 24 P-38s each. The three *Gruppen* of JG 77 claimed 72 P-38s, with III./JG 77 being credited with 30 of them. II./JG 51 claimed 58 P-38s, ranking it third among single *Gruppe*.

Not surprisingly, given their greater opportunities for combat with the P-38 groups, several Bf 109 pilots claimed more Lightnings shot down than their American

Pilots of the 49th FS/14th FG who claimed Bf 109s shot down during the fierce air battles over Sicily and southern Italy in the summer of 1943. They are, from left to right, 1Lt Anthony Evans (four Bf 109 victories), 2Lt Wayne Manlove (four Bf 109 victories) and 1Lts Lloyd Desmoss (three Bf 109 victories), Marlow Leikness (five Bf 109 victories) and Carroll Knott (three Bf 109 victories). (3A-28854, RG 342FH, NARA)

counterparts' claims for Bf 109s. The leading scorer was Hauptmann Franz Schiess with 17 claims, followed by Feldwebel Hans Feyerlein and Oberfeldwebel Otto Schultz-Wittner, with ten each.

The disparity, and the challenge, comes in the analysis of losses. In their monumental study of the air war over the Mediterranean (see Further Reading), Christopher Shores and his colleagues made every effort to document Allied and Axis claims and losses on a daily basis. In some cases, it is clear that a P-38 was lost in combat with Bf 109s and vice-versa, but in other cases the loss is attributed to combat with 'enemy fighters'.

It is possible, however, by looking at the times of action, the type of aircraft shot down and the claims of Allied and Axis units to make an approximation of losses, with a heavy emphasis on 'approximation'. Both Allied and Axis pilots overclaimed the number of aircraft they actually shot down, but it appears that there is less disparity between claims for P-38s and actual P-38 losses by the Bf 109 *Gruppen* than for claims by the Lightning groups for Bf 109s shot down and actual Bf 109 losses.

Bf 109 pilots claimed some 360 P-38s shot down. An analysis of the relevant volumes in the *Mediterranean Air War* series suggests that German pilots shot down approximately 183 P-38s. In contrast, the P-38 groups claimed 345 Bf 109s shot down, while the actual Bf 109 losses may have been somewhere in the region of 55–60 aircraft. It is quite possible that Bf 109 losses to P-38s were greater. Bf 109s described as 'lost in combat with B-17s' may actually have fallen victim to the escorting P-38s. Still, based on the most recent research, it is likely that the relationship between Bf 109 and P-38 losses remains heavily in favor of the German fighter. The question is, why was there this great disparity in results?

A plausible explanation lies in the combat tactics the Lightning groups employed in their main mission (escorting the bombers), the flying characteristics of the P-38 and the different levels of experience between American and German pilots – in his monograph on Lightnings of the Twelfth Air Force (see Further Reading), Tomasz Szlagor came to a similar conclusion. The doctrine of close escort tied the P-38s to the bomber formations. Invariably, as noted earlier, this gave the Bf 109s the initiative in the attack. Mission reports speak repeatedly of Bf 109s attacking with an altitude advantage, diving down on the P-38s at high speed and breaking away sharply after a firing pass. With its comparatively poorer roll rate, the P-38 was not well-suited to this kind of combat.

Capt Bob Davidson, who flew P-38s in North Africa with the 350th FG on intercept missions during 1943, and who participated in many mock combats with other Allied fighter types, had this to say about the Lightning:

When it came to the hard, fast, "slam bang" maneuvers of combat in Europe, the '38 was disappointing. Its big wingspan and slow initial reaction to aileron forces didn't allow it to change directions fast enough to compete on even terms with enemy aircraft. Once in a turn, with the combat flaps down, the P-38 could turn very tightly and hold its own against any fighter then in combat except the Spitfire IX. However, one just doesn't stay in a turn for very long when you're being out-turned and there's a bullet for the loser. So, the Luftwaffe fighters would utilize their rolling ability and break away from the P-38.

Tied to the bomber formations and less able to quickly roll away from an attacking fighter, roll into the attack or even pursue an enemy fighter, P-38 pilots were at a disadvantage. It may also be possible that a Lightning pilot firing at a Bf 109, seeing hits on the enemy fighter and then seeing his quarry break away, would have assumed to have shot it down.

There is also the matter of experience. As can be seen from the list of Bf 109 pilots with numerous claims against P-38s, these were men who were veterans of aerial combat and who, prior to meeting the Lightning for the first time, had been flying in the frontline for 18 months or longer. In contrast, their American opponents entered combat without experience. USAAF policy in North Africa was to pull a pilot out of combat when he had completed 50 missions. Many returned home to train newer pilots, who benefited from their experience. Sometimes this meant a new influx of inexperienced pilots into the squadrons. During April 1943, for example, the 95th FS received 25 replacement pilots – nine became casualties within their first month. As the war went on, and more and more of the *Experten* were lost in combat and Luftwaffe pilot training declined in quality, the situation was reversed.

Nevertheless, the importance of the Lightning as an escort fighter in the Mediterranean is without question. As Capt Davidson commented, the P-38s "were there when needed and couldn't be disregarded by the enemy when they went after the bombers. Regardless of the P-38's drawbacks and limitations as a fighter, anything that was reasonably maneuverable and could deliver the firepower of a P-38 was not to be ignored".

Although the Lightning groups may not have shot down as many Bf 109s as they claimed, and they had to absorb heavy losses at times, they succeeded admirably in defending the bombers. There are many variables that need to be taken into consideration when comparing the loss rates endured by bomb groups in the European and Mediterranean Theaters of Operations – the quality and quantity of German

Hauptmann Werner Schroer commanded II./JG 27 during the defense of Sicily and Italy. He had claimed his first victory in April 1941 flying with 1./JG 27 and later commanded 8./JG 27, before being promoted to *Gruppenkommandeur* of II./JG 27 in April 1943. Shortly after his promotion, Schroer claimed two P-38s shot down on April 29 for his 61st and 62nd claims. He was credited with three more Lightnings in May, and would go on to claim a further three P-38s during Defense of the Reich operations in 1944. (Tony Holmes Collection)

Regardless of the actual number of Axis fighters the P-38 groups shot down, their greatest contribution to the Allied success in the Mediterranean Theater of Operations was the protection they provided American medium and heavy bombers during their successful aerial interdiction campaigns over Tunisia, Sicily and Italy. During 1943, loss rates for Twelfth Air Force heavy bomber groups were consistently lower than those for the Eighth Air Force. These B-17Fs, from the 347th BS/99th BG, were photographed flying over the Mediterranean en route to a target in southern Italy during the summer of 1943. (3A-22820, NARA)

fighters, their tactics, the capabilities of Allied bombers under attack and the availability of fighter escort. It is noteworthy, however, that during the time the P-38 groups spent as part of the Twelfth Air Force, the loss rates for the heavy bomber units they escorted all the way to the target and back were considerably lower than the loss rates for heavy bomber units in the European Theater of Operations. The Twelfth Air Force learned at an earlier stage than the Eighth Air Force the critical need for escort fighters.

In combat after combat, Axis fighters rarely managed to inflict heavy losses on American bombers thanks to their P-38 escorts. The NASAF's success in interdicting Axis supplies to Tunisia and devastating Axis air strength in Sicily and Italy was due in no small measure to the Lightning pilots. Their sacrifice was not in vain.

Oberleutnant Franz Schiess, *Staffelkapitän* of 8./JG 53, and Oberleutnant Hans Roehrig, *Staffelkapitän* of 9./JG 53, share a joke at Comiso at the end of May 1943. By this point Schiess had already claimed ten P-38s shot down, while Roehrig had been credited with three. The latter would claim two more on July 11, 1943 (taking his overall tally to 74 victories), before being shot down and killed by Spitfires over Sicily 48 hours later. (2011-06-25_image_009_01, John Lambert Collection, MoF)

Leading P-38 pilots with claims against the Bf 109 (11/42–8/43)

	Bf 109 Claims	Final Score	Squadron(s)
2Lt Louis E. Curdes	7	9	95th FS
1Lt William J. Sloan	6	12	96th FS
1Lt Richard A. Campbell	5	6	37th FS
1Lt Marlow J. Leikness	5	5	49th FS
Maj Joel A. Owens	5	5	27th FS/14th FG
1Lt Gerald L. Rounds	5	5	97th FS
2Lt Paul R. Cochran	4	5	49th FS/96th FS
1Lt Anthony Evans	4	4	49th FS
1Lt Daniel Kennedy	4	5	27th FS
2Lt Wayne M. Manlove	4	4	49th FS
Capt Newell O. Roberts	4	5	94th FS
1Lt Herman W. Visscher	4	5	97th FS

Leading Bf 109 pilots with claims against the P-38 (11/42–8/43)

	P-38 Claims	Claims Prior to First P-38 Claim	Final Score	Unit(s)
Hauptmann Franz Schiess	17	26	68	*Stab.*/JG 53 and 8./JG 53
Feldwebel Hans Feyerlein	10	1	17	6./JG 53
Oberfeldwebel Otto Schultz-Wittner	10	40	72	4./JG 51
Leutnant Willy Kientsch	9	15	47	6./JG 27
Feldwebel Anton Hafner	8	67	203	6./JG 51
Major Kurt Ubben	7	85	93	III./JG 53
Oberfeldwebel Rudolf Ehrenberger	6	28	47	6./JG 53
Oberleutnant Gustav Frielinghaus	6	63	69	11./JG 3
Hauptmann Friedrich-Karl Müller	5	101	139	I./JG 53
Oberleutnant Herbert Puschmann	5	37	54	6./JG 51
Oberleutnant Hans Roehrig	5	61	74	9./JG 53
Oberfeldwebel Herbert Rollwage	5	30	66	5./JG 53
Feldwebel Horst Schlick	5	11	26	1./JG 77
Hauptmann Werner Schroer	5	60	106	II./JG 27

AFTERMATH

The duels between the P-38 Lightning and the Bf 109 continued until the end of the war in Europe, but over a wider field of battle. On November 1, 1943, the USAAF activated the Fifteenth Air Force to participate in the Combined Bomber Offensive against Germany. The Fifteenth took over control of the heavy and medium bomber

The P-38F/Gs with the three Lightning groups in the Mediterranean Theater of Operations soldiered on well into 1944. 94th FS/1st FG P-38F-15 43-2166 bares an impressive scoreboard of escort and dive-bombing missions and three kill markings for claims against Luftwaffe aircraft. Its hardworking groundcrew appear to be more impressed by a recent battle damage repair job, however. (3A-23512, RG 342FH, NARA)

units of the Ninth and Twelfth Air Forces (the medium bombers were soon returned to the Twelfth, however) and the three P-38 fighter groups.

With their long range, the Lightnings could escort the bombers to targets deep within southern Germany, Austria and central Europe. While the Eighth Air Force decided to standardize on a single fighter type in the form of the Merlin-engined P-51 (with the exception of the P-47 Thunderbolt-equipped 56th FG) and converted its P-38 fighter groups to the Mustang, the Fifteenth was happy to retain the three Lightning groups alongside four groups of Mustangs. The final battle between a P-38 and a Bf 109 took place on April 2, 1945, when 1Lt Samuel Lyons of the 27th FS claimed a Bf 109 northeast of Vienna.

The Bf 109 remained in production until Germany's surrender in May 1945. Delays in producing more capable jet fighters forced the Luftwaffe to rely on the Bf 109 longer than expected. Production of the Bf 109G-6 continued well into 1944. From the middle of 1943, Messerschmitt replaced the 20mm MG 151 cannon with the 30mm MK 108 cannon, which became standard with all subsequent models.

A small number were re-engined with the DB 605AS, which featured a larger supercharger giving a boost in maximum speed. The Bf 109G-14 incorporated many of the changes introduced on the later G-6 model. The G-14 used the DB 605AM engine, which had MW-50 methanol/water injection, and some had the DB 605AS. The Bf 109G-10 was an effort to bring older G-6 and G-14 models up to the standard of the final variant, the Bf 109K-4, which, thanks to its methanol/water injection, could attain a maximum speed of 441mph at 29,527ft.

This Bf 109G-4 or G-6 was shot down over the Anzio beachhead in early 1944. Following the successful invasion of Italy in September 1943, the Luftwaffe never seriously contested Allied air superiority over Italy again. Instead, more and more of the *Jagdgruppen* in the Mediterranean were brought back to Germany for Defense of the Reich operations. (Losses-Germany-Aircraft, Box 255, RG 208AA, NARA)

Thanks to these upgrades, the Bf 109 remained a dangerous adversary when flown to its strengths, but the quality of Luftwaffe pilots steadily declined as the war progressed. A catastrophic shortage of fuel cut training time to a bare minimum. The *Jagdgruppen* had fewer and fewer *Experten* and more and more poorly trained young pilots and former bomber pilots who had minimal experience flying fighters. By the middle of 1944, only two-thirds of the pilots in the Luftwaffe fighter force could be considered operationally ready.

The P-38 fighter groups, in contrast, received more capable Lightnings and better trained pilots. During 1944, the three P-38 groups received the new J- and L-models, which addressed several of the problems found in the earlier F-, G- and H-models. For the P-38J and subsequent models, Lockheed designed a new chin intake below the engine that housed a larger oil cooler and an improved intercooler system. This enabled P-38 pilots to take advantage of the Allison V-1750-89/91 engine's full 1,475hp at altitude, boosting the top speed to 414mph. Fuel tanks replaced the intercoolers in the wing leading edge, increasing the Lightning's range.

The P-38J-25 and P-38L started to reach units in Europe towards the end of 1944. These versions had electrically-operated dive brakes to deal with the problem of compressibility and a hydraulically powered aileron boost system that greatly improved the Lightning's roll rate. The P-38s could now take on the latest models of the Bf 109 and Fw 190 with greater confidence. The replacement pilots flying these aircraft into combat now had more than double the flying hours of their Luftwaffe counterparts, and often more than three to four times the number of hours in operational aircraft. The Luftwaffe no longer had the means to seriously challenge Allied air superiority.

During 1944, the Lightning groups, now with the Fifteenth Air Force, re-equipped with the improved P-38J and, later, the P-38L. These models helped limit the dangers posed to pilots from compressibility and greatly improved the P-38's roll rate, as well as providing more power at altitude. These Lightnings from the 1st FG's 27th FS are climbing in formation, with P-38L 44-24217 in the foreground, during an escort mission in November 1944. (3A-22848, RG 342FH, NARA)

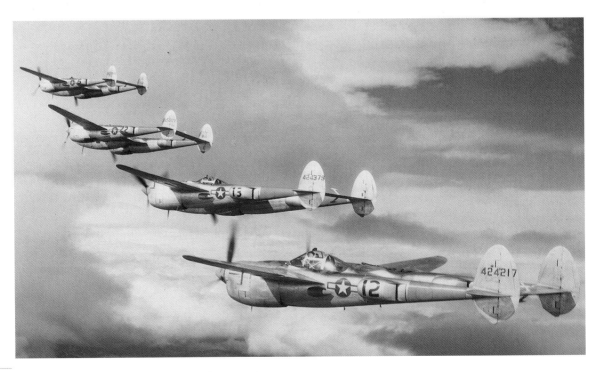

FURTHER READING

Blake, Steve, *Lightning Strikes – The Lockheed P-38* (Fonthill Media, 2020)

Blake, Steve, *Osprey Aircraft of the Aces 108 – P-38 Lightning Aces of the 82nd Fighter Group* (Osprey Publishing, 2012)

Blake, Steve with John Stanaway, *Adorimini ("Up and at 'Em!') – A History of the 82nd Fighter Group in World War II* (82nd Fighter Group History, Inc., 1992)

Bodie, Warren, *The Lockheed P-38 Lightning* (Widewing Publications, 1991)

Davidson, Bob, "Fork-Tailed Legend: Flying the P-38 Lightning", *Air Power*, Vol. 2, No. 6 (November 1972)

Fernandez-Sommerau, Marco, *Messerschmitt Bf 109 Recognition Manual – A Guide to Variants, Weapons and Equipment* (Classic Publications, 2004)

Green, William, *Augsburg Eagle – The Messerschmitt Bf 109*, (Aston Publications, 1987)

Ilfrey, Jack with Mark Copeland, *Happy Jack's Go Buggy – A Fighter Pilot's Story* (Schiffer Publishing, 1998)

Lambert, John W., *The 14th Fighter Group in World War II* (Schiffer Publishing, 2008)

Molesworth, Carl, *Osprey Duel 38 – P-40 Warhawk vs Bf 109 MTO 1942-44* (Osprey Publishing, 2011)

Mullins, John D., *An Escort of P-38s – The 1st Fighter Group in World War II* (Phalanx, 1995)

Olynyk, Frank, *Stars & Bars – A tribute to the American fighter ace 1920–1973* (Grub Street, 1995)

Prien, Jochen, Gerhard Stemmer, Peter Rodeike and Winfried Bock – *Die Jagdfliegerverbände der Deutschen Luftwaffe: Tiel 11/I and II: Einsatz im Mittelmeerraum, 1.1.bis 31.12.1943* (Buchverlag Rogge GmbH, 2010)

Prien, Jochen, *Jagdgeschwader 53 – A History of the "Pik As" Geschwader, May 1942–January 1944* (Schiffer Publishing, 1998)

Rein, Christopher M., *The North African Air Campaign – US Army Air Forces from El Alamein to Salerno* (University Press of Kansas, 2012)

Roba, Jean-Louis and Martin Pegg, *Luftwaffe Colours Volume 4 Section 2 – Jagdwaffe: The Mediterranean 1942–1943* (Classic Colours, 2003)

Roba, Jean-Louis and Martin Pegg, *Luftwaffe Colours Volume 4 Section 4 – Jagdwaffe: The Mediterranean 1943–1945* (Classic Colours, 2004)

Scutts, Jerry, *Osprey Aircraft of the Aces 2 – Bf 109 Aces of North Africa and the Mediterranean* (Osprey Publishing, 1994)

Shores, Christopher and Giovanni Massimello with Russell Guest, Frank Olynyk and Winfried Bock, *A History of the Mediterranean Air War 1940–1945: Volume Three – Tunisia and the End in Africa November 1942–May 1943* (Grub Street, 2016)

Shores, Christopher and Giovanni Massimello with Russell Guest, Frank Olynyk, Winfried Bock and Wg Cdr Andy Thomas, *A History of the Mediterranean Air War 1940–1945: Volume Four – Sicily and Italy to the Fall of Rome 14 May 1943 – 5 June 1944* (Grub Street, 2018)

Stanaway, John, *Osprey Aircraft of the Aces 19 – P-38 Lightning Aces of the ETO /MTO* (Osprey Publishing, 1998)

Steinhoff, Johannes, *Messerschmitts Over Sicily* (The Nautical & Aviation Publishing Company, 1987)

Szlagor, Tomasz – *Lightnings of the US 12th Army Air Force* (Kagero, 2009)

Weal, John, *Osprey Aviation Elite Units 12 – Jagdgeschwader 27 'Afrika'* (Osprey Publishing, 2003)

Weal, John, *Osprey Aviation Elite Units 22 – Jagdgeschwader 51 'Molders'* (Osprey Publishing, 2006)

Weal, John, *Osprey Aviation Elite Units 25 – Jagdgeschwader 53 'Pik-As'* (Osprey Publishing, 2007)

INDEX